No Youth Worker
Is an Island

NO YOUTH WORKER IS AN ISLAND

RIDGE BURNS
AND PAM CAMPBELL

VICTOR BOOKS

A DIVISION OF SCRIPTURE PRESS PUBLICATIONS INC.
USA CANADA ENGLAND

Copy Editor: Michael Kendrick
Cover Design: Mardell Ayres

Produced by the Livingstone Corporation

TABLE OF CONTENTS

This book is dedicated to the men of the Tuesday morning Bible study:

Brad Hanson	Phil Kavanagh
Tom Courtney	Jim Blower
Tom Hansen	Steve Larson
Rich Wegner	Mark Bauer
Chuck Kanoy	

These men have kept me from being an island.

Ridge Burns

For Herb Border.

Pam Campbell

Youth ministry can sometimes be a lonely job.

It can be lonely when you look around and notice you are the only adult in the entire room.

It can be lonely when the kids you worked so hard to build relationships with graduate and move on.

It can be lonely when you are being criticized unfairly by parents or members of the church staff.

It can be lonely when you are having a tough time coming up with that inspiring and entertaining program idea for tonight's youth group meeting.

It can be lonely when you do come up with an inspiring and entertaining program, but the kids don't show up for it.

It can be lonely when you feel like you must be the only youth minister in the world who isn't a personal friend of Tony Campolo.

It can be lonely when you try to identify all the "results" your youth ministry has produced over the last year.

It can be lonely when you hear how much money other people—with your age, education, and experience—are making.

It can be lonely when you try that incredible new idea and it backfires on you, and your kids rebel.

It can be lonely when you are trying to help others grow spiritually, but your own spiritual life is going in the dumpster.

It can be lonely when you wish you had a few adult friends.

If you've ever felt a bit lonely in youth ministry, you'll appreciate this extraordinary book by Ridge Burns and Pam Campbell.

It's not a book on how to make friends or how to eliminate loneliness. But after you read it, I know you'll feel like you've made a couple of new friends, and I don't think you'll feel quite so alone.

Ridge Burns has become very well known in youth ministry

circles—not because he is an expert youth worker with all the answers—but because he has integrity, credibility, and a true servant's heart. Ridge is not only well known, but well loved by everyone who knows him, including me.

Personally, what I love most about Ridge is his sensitivity to others. He really cares about people. This quality is undoubtedly what led him to create an organization that serves homeless people on the streets of America's biggest cities.

On more than one occasion, I have received a phone call out of the blue from Ridge, just to offer a few words of encouragement or to let me know he was praying for me. When you know someone like Ridge Burns, it's hard to feel too terribly alone.

It's that kind of caring that also led Ridge and Pam to write this book. This is not another book full of program ideas and activities for your youth group. It's not a book that offers another philosophy for effective youth ministry. Instead, this book is like a having a heart-to-heart talk with a good friend. Sure, there's practical help, good ideas, and wise counsel in this book, but more important, there's empathy, understanding, encouragement, and honesty. *No Youth Worker Is An Island* is a book that will make you feel better after you read it, not worse.

After all, isn't that what friends are for?

Wayne Rice
Founder, Youth Specialties

*"No man is an island, entire of itself;
every man is a piece of the continent, a part
of the main."*

John Donne
"Devotions upon Emergent Occasions"

No youth worker is an island. The perception that we are alone is not necessarily a reality. We just *think* we're alone. Like the prophet who hid in a cave.

Elijah achieved great success against the prophets of Baal on Mount Carmel, but when he heard that Queen Jezebel was out to kill him, he ran for his life. As he hid in a mountain cave, the Lord sent a great wind, an earthquake, and a fire. Then came a gentle whisper from the Lord, asking Elijah what he was doing in the cave. Elijah replied:

> *"I have been very zealous for the Lord God Almighty. The Israelites have rejected your covenant, broken down your altars, and put your prophets to death with the sword. I am the only one left, and now they are trying to kill me too" (1 Kings 19:14).*

God responded by telling Elijah to return to His work with the Israelites. He went on to say that He had reserved "seven thousand in Israel—all whose knees have not bowed down to Baal and all whose mouths have not kissed him" (1 Kings 19:18).

How often we youth workers experience the highs and lows Elijah must have felt in his ministry. We too feel zealous for

God. We too are depressed and frustrated by students who reject us and the Gospel. Sometimes we even feel as if parents and unhappy church members are trying to kill us.

Yet we must listen closely to God's message—get back to work and remember that we are not alone in our ministry. Just as Elijah was mistaken in his conclusion that he alone had remained faithful, we are mistaken in assuming that we are alone.

Take a look at the stories Ridge has woven in the chapters of this book. The 100 youth workers (professional and lay people, salaried and volunteer, young and old) we surveyed for this book share many of the same challenges, frustrations, and dreams. These chapters summarize our research and responses to these important concerns of youth ministry. In each chapter, you'll find a statistical summary of our survey, stories from Ridge's ministry experience, a Small Church Spotlight from my perspective, and a Scripture meditation.

Youth ministry can be a lonely calling. But you're not alone, so forget the note in the bottle. Try the time-tested advice in this book instead.

Pam Campbell
May 1992

No Youth Worker
Is an Island

STUDENTS

You and Students

	Strongly Disagree	Disagree	Somewhat Disagree	Undecided	Agree	Somewhat Agree	Strongly Agree
I have a pretty good understanding of the thoughts and feelings of each individual in my group.	1	4	9	4	24	43	15
Several of my students need more counseling than I can provide.	1	5	8	5	19	39	23
It's hard to keep many of my group members interested in spiritual things.	0	12	17	7	31	24	9
I try to maintain regular one-on-one contact with each group member.	1	7	10	3	21	40	18
Most of my group members feel free to discuss any problem with me.	1	1	6	11	34	40	7
My group as a whole would be stronger if I could control a handful of "trouble" students.	11	23	20	12	12	16	5

Figures have been rounded to the nearest whole percentage.

Summary

According to George Barna, 20 million people in 1990 were teenagers in the 13 to 18 age bracket (7.9% of the total population).[1] The most pressing issue by far in the minds of teens is having goals or a purpose for their lives. Their next concerns are related to fears about the future, security, and relationships.[2]

Most youth workers surveyed (82%) believe they understand 13 to 18 year olds and can relate well to them. They (81%) also believe that students feel free to seek their advice on any number of problems. At the same time, 81% say they are unequipped to handle the counseling demands of their students.

In this chapter, Ridge describes many students with differing backgrounds and needs with whom he has had relationships—both healthy and unhealthy. As you think about individual students, ask yourself:

➤ Do I really know my students? Are there students I'd rather not know?

➤ Am I dealing with the specific needs of my students?

➤ Do I treat all students equally?

Youth Workers Speak:

"I like to see kids mature into Christian people—the joy and energy of kids as they get excited about spiritual growth."

Youth ministry exists because of the perception that youth workers are able to impact the lives of students. Our task is to challenge students to bring their behavior, lifestyle, and commitment in line with the attitude of Christ. We are daily exploring ways to influence students. But I wonder how many of us consider how students are influencing and impacting *our* lives.

I think it's time for those of us in youth ministry to take a close look at how students influence our lives. I'm willing to admit that there are three major areas where my life is greatly impacted by kids: affirmation, loyalty, and space.

I expect affirmation from kids. My ego is fragile, so I need them to tell me how much they like me. As I look at the shelves in my office, I see some examples of how important such affirmation is to me. On one shelf is a craft made by a student at summer camp. On another shelf is a bracelet from Mexico and a little Canadian flag—"thank-you" souvenirs from mission trips. Those items remind me of the importance I place on affirmation from students.

I also expect loyalty. No, I don't tell students not to go to other youth groups. But I get very disappointed, for example, when a student goes with another group on a retreat. I want him or her to say, "No, I already belong to a youth group, and we're doing something else that weekend." Maybe instead of commitment cards, handshakes, and hugs, I ought to have my youth group tattooed.

I also need my own space. I want students to be close to me, but I want to set boundaries on those relationships. I want to be able to maintain a certain distance from students. I don't really want a student to know my daily schedule because I'm afraid he or she will limit my flexibility. I want the right to say no to students simply because they're inconveniencing me.

It scares me a little to see how badly I want affirmation and to what lengths I will go to hear students applaud. I don't like feeling jealous of other youth pastors who are ministering to my kids, but I have a hard time making those feelings go away. And my need for space sometimes gets distorted because I overcommit myself. As a result, individual kids get shortchanged.

Kids influence me both positively and negatively. Yet, all these influences can work for good in my life. And the kinds of kids I talk about in this chapter have shaped my ministry and my effectiveness as a youth pastor.

Clingers

I have always been bothered and troubled by kids who liked me more than I liked them. You know, the kids who come to your youth group and try to build relationships with everyone else, but for some reason they can't quite build those relationships. So they come to you because, after all, you are paid to talk to them. They want a ride home, they want to sit next to you on the bus, they want to eat lunch with you at the retreat. They dominate your time and prevent you from getting to know other kids with whom you really want and need to build relationships.

Clingers have always been hard for me. I've been rude and cold to them. I haven't been the kind of youth pastor that God has called me to be. If God has called me to be the youth pastor at the church, I want to have a ministry with all of the kids. But Clingers are very difficult for me to minister to.

I had just finished a long day—a breakfast Bible study with kids before school, a campus visit, and a ballgame after school. Now it was time for our regular youth meeting on Wednesday night. As the time came for students to arrive, the first person in the door was Rick.

Rick was a Clinger who loved to spend time with me, and I really needed to spend more time with him. But he was a hard kid with a lot of problems—a bad family situation, a bad academic record in school, low ranking in the popularity poll. Rick had no place else to go to get loved and cared for except the church, and as the youth pastor, I knew that.

Still, I sure had a hard time loving him and spending time with him because it seemed that he would never let me go. He was always by my side, always standing with me, always right next to me.

As the meeting door swung closed, Rick rushed over to tell me a problem that he told me about last week and to ask for more advice on how to solve it. After I talked briefly with him, other kids arrived and I began the meeting.

Then, during one of the games, Rick came over and told me about the same problem. By this time I was getting irritated and just wanted to enjoy the rest of the kids in the youth group.

After the youth meeting, of course Rick didn't have a ride home. So I ended up sitting in his driveway (as I had for the last four or five weeks), hearing about his same problems over and over again. All I could think about was how he was dominating my time and I wished I was with someone else.

I have big problems with Clingers. I admit that down deep in my spirit, while he was pouring out his heart, I wanted to be anywhere else but listening to this guy.

So how do I deal with Clingers?

First, I try to express compassion to all kids in my youth ministry. My heart needs to be broken for these kids that cling and overload me with their needs. I need to care for them. With Rick, I realized I needed to spend some time with him and that he really was a lost sheep.

Second, I've learned to confront Clingers. In Rick's case, I needed to talk him about the way he was dominating my time and preventing other kids with needs from spending time with me. In fact, I got together with Rick after school one day and told him that I felt we had a problem. I explained that he was taking up a lot of my time and was not allowing other kids to talk to me one-on-one. I asked him if he could see it as part of his ministry to allow others access to me. To my surprise, Rick viewed that as a very positive idea and realized he could allow other kids a little more space.

The third thing I need to do is schedule a regular time to meet with Clingers. When I set up regular meetings with Rick, he realized that I was not just abandoning him, but that I was offering him an opportunity to have some personal time with me. As we met on a weekly basis, I began to see that Rick had some needs that I could not fulfill, so I referred him to one of our associate staff people in the counseling area. This suggestion seemed to satisfy Rick's needs.

The fourth thing I've learned from Clingers is that they really like me and see something in me that they think can really help them. Rick's particular circumstance allowed him to find the love and help he was seeking. His heart was soft, and he viewed me as a person who could help him. That realization helped me to see him positively.

Winners

I admit it. I like Winners better than Losers. I like kids who are positive and athletic, who are leaders on campus, who reach their potential, and who come from good families. I have a natural inclination toward them. I don't have to work at liking kids that win.

Charlie and Carol were Winners. Charlie was kind of a floppy, funny soccer goalie who wasn't the best at what he did, but he came from a good family and wanted to do great things for God. Carol was a cheerleader who had the lead in the school musical and led worship at our church. Charlie and Carol will probably succeed at whatever they do.

I like people like that. In fact, I like them so much that it causes some problems for kids who don't win. When I play favorites, it prevents kids who are Losers from getting close to me. I recognize that my high regard for Winners speaks louder than my care for people who don't win.

So how do I deal with Winners?

First, I must admit that it's easy to work with Winners. I know that when I give projects to students with good self-esteem and positive attitudes, those students will turn those projects into reality with little or no help from me. They have the self-discipline and self-motivation to work.

Second, I realize that Winners make me look good. I can write books, give seminars, and talk to people about the Winners to whom I've ministered—all because these students make me look good as a youth pastor. I gravitate toward Winners so I can feed my own ego. But I also gravitate toward Winners because they are the trophies of my ministry that I share with others.

Third, I've come to realize that it's the Winners who can fake me out. The kids who are struggling with problems are usually up front with me. They tell me exactly what's going on with their lives. I don't have to go through any smoke screens in order to find out what their real needs are. But many times I discover later on in life that the Winners were fooling me during my entire ministry with them.

This happened with one student whom I really believed in (and held up as an example of sexual purity). Ten years after my ministry with her, I found out that she was as promiscuous as some of the other kids in the youth group. However, she had this winning attitude about her that prevented me seeing through her protective shell. I found out that Winners are sometimes the hardest kids to reach for Christ because they can get things done *without* the strength of God.

For me, the way to work with Winners is to put them in non-Winner roles. For example, Jeff was the president of his high school student body. He had a lot of influence on campus, and

23

his opinion carried a lot of weight in the youth group. When it came time to select the students who would lead our next mission trip, naturally Jeff's name surfaced to the top.

The selection of student leadership was done not by election, but by the students who led the previous year's mission trip. Even though Jeff would have been a good leader, the consensus was that he was already in a lot of leadership roles and that he needed to learn how to be a follower.

Jeff really struggled with that decision, and at first, he determined not to go on the trip. But when he found out his friends were going (as well as some other people with whom he wanted to spend time), he decided to go on the trip anyway. That experience as a follower caused him to learn some things about himself that he wouldn't have learned had he been a trip leader. I've learned to put Winners like Jeff in situations where they have the potential to be Losers, and where they have to draw their strength from God instead of from their own natural resources.

Losers

I am not a naturally empathic person. I don't find myself drawn to students who have problems. If I have a choice between making an appointment with a kid who is working on a project and a hurting kid who wants to talk about a problem, I'll pick the first kid every time. I feel more equipped to handle projects and tasks than kids who need help on a long-term basis.

My natural tendency is to try to rescue kids, fix their problems, and get them back on the road to tasks *as soon as I can.* That's how I'm wired, and often that becomes a problem for me. Kids who are losing and struggling in life find it difficult to relate to my personality. They don't usually seek me out.

A kid once came up to me and said, "Ridge, for the two years that I've known you, I've carried this problem. But I felt like you were only interested in the kids who really wanted to accomplish something for God. I'm not whole, so I can't accomplish anything for God." What an indictment on how I relate to kids!

Brian was one such kid. He was insecure and a terrible student. He was also from a divorced family and didn't relate very well to his stepfather. His mom was frustrated and didn't know what to do. I got together with Brian and his family every week. Brian, his stepfather, and his mom talked over simple problems like cleaning his room, doing his homework, going to school, getting a job. But for some reason, Brian couldn't get through the basics of daily life and become a functioning member of his family. In fact, his mom's highest goal for Brian was simply to get him to graduate from high school. So I made a commitment to help Brian graduate.

I didn't really like Brian. He went on a mission trip with us and for some reason he showed up at the last training meeting with his head shaved, thinking it showed his commitment to God and to the group. But all it did was make him look silly, so he wore a bandana for the first few days of the mission trip until he got comfortable with his new appearance. Brian was a troubled kid, and he had difficulty relating to me. When I talked with Brian, I found myself struggling with just trying to be a friend to him.

So how do I deal with Losers?

First of all, I admit I need some people in my life who don't fit into my stereotype of what winning is all about. Kids who aren't winning in life, who have habits of making wrong decisions, help balance my life. I would be unbalanced if God didn't give me a ministry to kids who constantly make wrong choices.

Second, Losers allow me to see God's power. One of the ways I was able to help Brian become more of a Winner was by challenging him in an area that bothered me and other students. Brian was perpetually late for our mission trip training sessions. After a while, his tardiness became an issue with the rest of the students in training. *We've got enough self-discipline to get here on time,* they thought, *so how come Brian can't do the same?*

I gave Brian a last warning about being late. Then I put him in charge of timekeeping on the entire mission trip. He was responsible for waking students and making sure they arrived on time at their assigned work sites. He essentially became in charge of the area where he was weakest.

Students resented Brian because he was always late, but when they discovered he could encourage them to be on time, he became a Winner. Sometimes the very issues that cause kids to be Losers can be used to help them become more in tune with what God has for them to do.

Do you know where Brian is today? He is ministering in the Midwest full-time, on fire for God, doing great things for Him. I had very little to do with it. Another sponsor in our church took Brian under his wing, saw his potential, and listened to his problems.

I look at Brian ministering for God, and I cannot believe it. When I talk about kids who are Losers, I'm not talking about kids who have hurts in their lives and then move on. I'm talking about kids who constantly make wrong choices. They don't have a support structure, but when God rearranges their lives, it's unbelievable to watch the joy that takes place.

Defectors

Have you ever had a kid leave your youth group and start attending another youth group? Have you ever had a student come to your office and say, "I'm no longer going to be part of your ministry because I've decided that the youth group down the street is a little bit better"?

Carl left my youth ministry. Carl was a great student and the star quarterback of the high school football team. In fact, he was the number-one quarterback in the state. But this popular kid decided he would rather go to another youth group in town. When Carl left my youth group, he didn't tell me he was leaving. I got the news that he had left at the local youth pastors' meeting when another youth pastor came to me and said, "How do you feel about Carl coming to my youth group?"

My first reaction was embarrassment. I was embarrassed that I did not have the charismatic leadership to keep this prize kid in my youth group. (Notice how my bias toward Winners was affecting me again.) The fact that I couldn't keep Carl seemed to indicate that I was an ineffective leader. I was also angry that Carl would dare go somewhere else for ministry. I found myself gossiping about Carl and his attitudes toward our youth group.

"Oh, he didn't give us a fair chance. He never gave us enough time. He was never really committed anyway."

But what I was really doing was trying to satisfy my own ego needs by suggesting that he didn't leave because of me. Actually, Carl left because his friends attended another church. He didn't have time to make new friendships, so he simply wanted to build spiritual relationships with the friends he was already hanging out with at school. Carl didn't leave because he didn't like me; he left because he liked his friends, and he wanted to worship and praise the Lord with them.

So how do I deal with Defectors?

When a kid leaves my youth group for another one, I am able to handle it a little bit better now. I first think about and then write out the reasons why the student left. By simply evaluating the student's reasons, I can accept his or her departure without taking it so personally.

Another thing I do is recognize that some kids leave the youth group because my ministry has somehow been ineffective. Sometimes I have a tendency to see only what I want to see in my ministry. But when a kid defects, I am forced to examine my ministry for any gaping holes. For example, some kids may leave the youth group because they aren't being ministered to. This painful situation may be one way that God is shouting that I need to improve my ministry.

This was certainly the case for me in terms of my evangelistic approach. Some kids in one of my youth groups were real evangelists and wanted to see kids come to know Christ. But I was so discipleship-oriented that these kids did not feel fulfilled in my youth group. When they left the group, I took it personally. I realized later that God was speaking to me through their action and that I needed to open up a new area of ministry in my youth group.

Agenda Carriers

I run a youth missions organization. My job is to get kids involved in ministry in the inner city. I am highly committed to providing kids with hands-on ministry experience. Yet I find that sometimes high school kids from my church carry their parents' agenda about what kinds of missions I should be involved with.

Beth invited me over for dinner one night. She said her parents wanted me to meet their family and spend a little time just talking together. It seemed like a nonthreatening situation. Little did I know that after dinner I would have to sit through two hours of slides showing Beth's summer experience with a teen mission organization.

As the evening progressed, Beth's parents made it clear that they felt I should direct kids toward missions organizations rather than try to provide a missions experience through our own programs at the church. In other words, Beth's parents had invited me over to their house simply to give me their opinions.

After this evening, I became uneasy with Beth. I did not want get together with her. I questioned and second-guessed every-thing she said to me to see if there were any hidden agendas.

At the same time, I realized that Beth evidently did have a great experience in the Philippines that summer. The things that took place in her life were the things I wanted to take place in every kid's life in our youth group. But the way that Beth's parents communicated that experience made me really angry toward their daughter. I could have handled the situation differently, but unfortunately I didn't.

So how do I deal with Agenda Carriers?

First of all, I've learned to separate the kid from the agenda the parents are addressing. Beth was a wonderful girl, and I could have really used her help in some areas of the youth ministry. Instead, I let my feelings get in the way.

Second, I talk to the student about his or her own feelings. Students shouldn't feel caught in the middle between me and their parents. Beth is not the only person in 15 years of ministry who has carried the mail for her parents. Still, each time this kind of conflict happens, I have trouble learning my lesson.

Third, I try to use the student's strengths to enhance my ministry. It's true that I struggled with Beth's tunnel vision, her inability to accept other types of mission experiences as valid. However, I knew she was missions-minded and had some skills that I really wanted to use in our youth group. Therefore, I involved Beth in running our missions conference, operating the soup kitchen, and organizing other programs. I cared about her involvement in missions, but I didn't have to be sold on the particular organization in which she was involved.

Fourth, I make sure I don't gather an army against the student. It would have been very easy to pit students who had equally rewarding missions experiences against Beth to invalidate or lessen the importance of her experience.

Burdensome Kids

Some kids are just difficult to minister to. They take a lot of work, effort, and time. They're not people with problems; they're just kids with special needs who require a lot of time. Lately I've come into contact with many kids who learn differently, who are dyslexic, or who participate in some kind of learning deficiency program.

Greg was in a wheelchair and required special attention for everything. On missions trips we had to help him in and out of the bathroom and showers. We had to rent special vehicles. It was difficult and time-consuming, but watching Greg minister to others was one of the greatest joys of my ministry.

So how do I deal with Burdensome Kids?

Some of the greatest rewards in ministry take the greatest amount of time. Kids who have special needs sometimes slow your ministry down to a pace where students can recognize what serving others is all about. When I think back on Greg, I think God used him to teach me and the youth group this lesson in servanthood.

Not long ago, I saw Greg in line at the Splash Mountain at Disneyland. There he was in his wheelchair, still looking the same after eight years. When I went over to say "Hi," Greg said, "Thank you for the time that was invested and for the time you spent with me."

I've come to realize that kids who have special needs are placed in my life by God for a reason. They round out my youth program and, perhaps, make me more sensitive to the needs of others. Many times those of us in fast-paced youth ministries need to be slowed down, and those kids who have special needs help us regain our perspective.

Second, I can build a team of students who care about Burdensome Kids. In this way I don't feel solely responsible. I need to delegate responsibility to kids who really want to help and share. Mark was one of those kids who wanted to help, so he took Greg under his wing. As a result of Mark's caring, he and Greg developed a deep friendship.

Third, I let the kid with a special need exercise leadership every once in a while. I remember the day Greg led a Bible study on one of our mission trips. From the broader platform of his wheelchair, he challenged the other kids to look at themselves in ways that I could not have done. For many kids, that Bible study was probably the most powerful experience of the entire trip.

Natural Attractors

I really enjoy the personalities of some kids. I like kids who are funny and have energy, even if they are discipline problems. If they're fun to be around, I find myself really drawn to them. They don't have to be Winners, valedictorians, or all-star athletes; they can just be fun kids.

Ken was one of those kids. Even though he played football, he really wasn't all that good. (His team sure wasn't very good!) But Ken was just a good guy to be around, and he loved to play tricks on people. I found myself spending a lot of time with him. I liked being around Ken, but it became a problem when I began to overlook some of his faults. Oh, he'd swear a little bit and get drunk a little bit on Friday nights. I found myself not talking to him about Jesus like I would with any other kid because I liked him, and he could reject what I shared in such a way that it was just funny.

Not only did I overlook his faults, but I began to show favoritism. Instead of getting involved with some of the kids who really needed my attention, I found myself drawn to Ken to hear his latest episode. Kids began to notice how much attention I gave Ken, so they began to act like him to get a share of my attention.

I also adopted another bad characteristic. I began using Ken and other kids I liked as shields against Clingers and Losers. By filling up my time with these kids that I liked, I had no time for the undesirable ones.

So how do I deal with Natural Attractors?

First of all, I've come to understand that ministry is serious business and, that sometimes, in order to accomplish ministry, I must deny myself the right of being with people I am naturally attracted to.

Second, I try be fairer to all students by admitting to myself that I am naturally drawn to some personality types more than others. At one church, I made a list of students in my youth group, ranking them in three categories: kids I really liked, kids I sort of liked, and kids I didn't like at all. Then I tried to think of ways I could reduce those distinctions.

Finally, I've noticed that when I am drawn to certain students, I tend to demand less from them. But just the opposite should be true. One way I've dealt with this problem is by writing behavioral objectives for those kids to whom I am particularly drawn. Written objectives help me be more conscious of the growth I want for those kids.

Disloyal Kids

I've noticed that kids do not have much loyalty these days. They drift from youth group to youth group depending on who has the best program and social events. I've taken polls on retreats and found out that half the kids go to other churches. They just happened to like the ski trip I planned better than their youth group's bowling night.

There is little or no evangelism taking place when kids bring their other Christian friends to social activities. These outsiders come to the activity to share in the fun but don't have anything to do with the regular times of group fellowship. That bothers me, but not as much as when I find out *my* kids are attending another youth pastor's summer camp or winter retreat.

This lack of loyalty and commitment not only makes me angry and hurt, but it breeds competition in my spirit. I feel less inclined to cooperate with churches where my kids are involved in their youth events. When I find out that another youth pastor may have something better than what I have, sometimes I display some very un-Christian attitudes.

So how do I deal with Disloyal Kids?

One of the ways that I have tried to deal with this issue is to cooperate in community-wide events involving several youth groups from the area. Not only do these large events allow my kids to mix with kids in other youth groups, but they force me to be in contact with the other youth pastors with whom I sometimes feel competition. Usually I find that they have the same kinds of feelings and fears about me that I have about them. As we talk about our fears and common experiences, we are able to handle them much better.

Small Church Spotlight

I had never worked with unchurched kids until I came to the small church I'm at now. Unlike Ridge, my ministry does not exist because parents perceive a spiritual need in their kids. In fact, some of the kids' parents resent my influence on their sons and daughters. They're afraid I'm going to turn their kids into religious fanatics.

It's difficult to impact the lives of unchurched students. The six to eight hours a week that I spend modeling Christ to a kid doesn't always compensate for the remaining hours spent with a mom or dad who could care less about Christ.

For example, I've done everything I know—whined, griped, threatened, bribed, enticed, blackmailed—to get Chris to attend the Sunday morning worship service. But Chris doesn't think she needs to go to church to be a Christian. Why? "Because Mom is a Christian and she doesn't attend church," Chris rationalizes. How can I challenge Chris to bring her behavior, lifestyle, and commitment in line with the attitude of Christ, rather than the primary authority figure (Mom) in her life?

I agonize over my inability to effect dramatic change in my unchurched students. I know God has put me here to reach those kids, but it's frustrating to see them assimilate their parents' values.

When I finally realized I didn't have to play the role of the Holy Spirit to these kids, my frustration and anxiety were reduced. You see, I thought part of my job description was to convict these kids about their lifestyles and attitudes. That's why I went to such extremes with threats, gripes, bribes, and emotional blackmail. Now I'm beginning to see that God has called me to reach those kids by modeling an alternative lifestyle and Christian values. Then it's up to them and the Holy Spirit to effect change.

Scripture Meditation

"My brothers, as believers in our glorious Lord Jesus Christ, don't show favoritism. Suppose a man comes into your meeting wearing a gold ring and fine clothes, and a poor man in shabby clothes also comes in. If you show special attention to the man wearing fine clothes and say, 'Here's a good seat for you,' but say to the poor man, 'You stand there' or 'Sit on the floor by my feet,' have you not discriminated among yourselves and become judges with evil thoughts?

"Listen, my dear brothers: Has not God chosen those who are poor in the eyes of the world to be rich in faith and to inherit the kingdom he promised those who love him? But you have insulted the poor. Is it not the rich who are exploiting you? Are they not the ones who are dragging you into court? Are they not the ones who are slandering the noble name of him to whom you belong?

"If you really keep the royal law found in Scripture, 'Love your neighbor as yourself,' you are doing right. But if you show favorit-

ism, you sin and are convicted by the law as lawbreakers. For whoever keeps the whole law and yet stumbles at just one point is guilty of breaking all of it. For he who said, 'Do not commit adultery,' also said, 'Do not murder.' If you do not commit adultery but do commit murder, you have become a lawbreaker.

"Speak and act as those who are going to be judged by the law that gives freedom, because judgment without mercy will be shown to anyone who has not been merciful. Mercy triumphs over judgment!" (James 2:1-13).

After reading the Scripture, spend some time meditating on what God has to say to you. Use the following questions to study this passage.

1. Why should believers not show favoritism?

2. What kinds of discrimination take place in your youth group?

3. Are you guilty of favoritism?

4. How have your acts of favoritism affected your students?

5. Think of one student against whom you've discriminated. How can you show mercy rather than judgment to this person in the future?

Father, help me to love and care for

_____ *as myself.*

(Insert the name of one student whom you've discriminated against.)

SCHOOL AND COMMUNITY

You and School/Community

	Strongly Disagree	Disagree	Somewhat Disagree	Undecided	Somewhat Agree	Agree	Strongly Agree
The pressures of school make it hard for my students to commit to youth group activities.	0	11	15	3	33	25	13
Many teachers/coaches promote values contrary to Christian teaching.	3	7	5	27	21	28	9
I go on campus regularly to see my group members "in their element."	8	23	14	7	15	10	23
I am welcomed on campus by school authorities whenever I want to visit.	8	14	7	30	10	17	14
I attend many of the extracurricular activities of my group members (games, concerts, etc.).	0	9	8	5	28	27	22
Most of my group members are just as open about their Christian beliefs at school as they are at church.	4	22	22	15	27	9	1
Our church has a good reputation in the community.	1	0	1	7	15	54	22

Figures have been rounded to the nearest whole percentage.

Summary

When asked about ministry on campus, youth workers surveyed were split in their answers, with 48% regularly visiting campus and 45% steering away from school visits. At the same time, 77% attended students' extracurricular activities.

In this chapter, Ridge talks about his ministry experiences on public and Christian school campuses and his relationships with teachers and coaches. As you check out our advice and comments, ask yourself:

➤ Should I be visiting my students' campus on a regular basis? Why or why not?

➤ How can I help students make their spiritual lives as transparent at school as they are at church?

➤ What kinds of relationships should I have with teachers and coaches?

Youth Workers Speak:

"School is not the place to do youth ministry. I consider it a privilege to be on campus and want to make my services available. But I think my ministry will fly without being on campus."

Whether the students in my youth group attend public, Christian, or parish schools . . . or whether the community they live in is rural, suburban, or inner-city. . . I must understand and interact with my students' primary environments. The major influences of school and community have a significant impact on my ministry to students. My role as a youth pastor is to help students interpret the influences of their campus and community and then find where Christ belongs among these influences.

Kids on Campus

Every church where I've been in ministry has expected me to go on campus to do contact work with kids. The problem is when I see kids at school, they act differently from every other time I'm with them. Kids who are open and trusting with me at church suddenly become closed and suspicious toward me at school.

Some kids really welcome my presence on campus. They seem so excited that I want to meet them on their turf and be part of their lives there. One such kid was Mike. Whenever I attended one of Mike's wrestling meets or football games, he always spent a few minutes talking with me after the event. He appreciated my presence, and I felt closer to him because he was willing to introduce me to his friends and coaches.

There's another large segment of students who don't want to see me outside of the church setting. It's almost as if I had invaded a hidden part of their lives, as if I shouldn't have known that they go to school. They're embarrassed to be seen with me on campus and want to make me feel as uncomfortable as possible. The worst thing that happens while I'm on campus is when kids ignore me. I see them duck behind buildings or hide behind their lockers just so they don't have to talk with me.

Lynn tried to avoid me at all costs whenever I was on campus. If she saw me at a ball game, she tried to ignore my wave. If she passed me in the hall, she nodded and rushed on past with her friends. I felt as if a wall was forming between us.

So how should I view kids on campus?

I've learned several things about going on campus. First of all, the school campus belongs to the students. It's their turf I am entering, and they need to feel that I respect the rules of their turf. That is, never push yourself on a student. In fact, I try to warn my students when I'll be on campus so I don't catch them by surprise.

I also need to realize I am an uninvited guest on the campus. To be quite honest, I'm not sure that contact work on campus during school days is all that effective. It seems to embarrass a lot more kids than it encourages.

Visiting a High School Campus

I always feel very insecure when I visit a high school campus. I'm afraid I'll go into the wrong building at the wrong time or walk across the sacred senior grass or violate some other school tradition and have to take the abuse for doing such a thing. I find myself meandering around campus, hoping that one of my kids will talk to me so I can prove I am needed on campus.

Being at a high school event makes me feel as if I'm a long way from the world of high school. Yet I have particularly enjoyed youth ministry when I go to events like football games or basketball games. The funny thing is that I think I have better opportunities to build relationships with the parents attending those high school events than I do with the kids who are attending or participating. The parents seem to be really excited about my presence. They want to talk to me about things at church and what their kids are doing.

So how do I go about visiting the high school campus?

One of the things that I've done each time I've moved to a new community is network with other adults or youth pastors who have good ministries on campus. I ask them to give me a tour of the high school campuses and introduce me to some of the teachers. That seems to help me break some of the ice.

Another thing that I've done is sign up for Parents' Observation Day at the local high school. Some high schools have a tour to orient the parents and help them feel more comfortable on campus. I found this to be very helpful at easing some of the anxiety *I* felt.

Teachers and Coaches

Talking with teachers and coaches is the worst! They cannot figure out why I would want to spend my time at a place they want to desert as soon as their last class is over. Whenever I am on a high school campus and meet one of the teachers, I feel a little awkward. I never know what to say. I particularly don't know whether to bring up the fact that I'm a youth pastor. I wonder how they will respond to a religious leader being on campus.

I hate meetings with coaches worse than teachers, particularly when a student has to miss a practice or two because he or she is going on a winter retreat or a mission trip. When I meet with a coach, I usually feel a sense of competition. Many coaches feel I'm trying to ruin their discipline of the team. With few exceptions, the public school teachers I've worked with have a pretty small worldview. And the church is definitely not part of their world. These conflicts make some of my conversations uncomfortable.

So how do I build bridges with teachers and coaches?

One way I have been successful in bettering relationships with teachers is by volunteering to drive a team to a sporting event or to chaperone a dance. Consistent, loyal support of sports activities usually doesn't go unnoticed by coaches and teachers. Occasionally I offer to help parents with the snack bar at sports events. Coaches and teachers seems to appreciate my willingness to serve in ways that are not required of me.

Finally, if teachers and coaches attend the church where I'm ministering, I try to get to know them on a personal level. I ask for their insights on students. Though I'm not sure they realize it, teachers and coaches seem to have almost as much influence as parents on students' self-esteem and life goals. By building relationships with some key teachers and coaches, I may be able to help them more fully understand their impact on students and why students' worldviews need to be broader than academics and sports.

Kids Who Go to Christian School

When I go on Christian school campuses, it's usually to conduct chapels. I'm uncomfortable speaking in their chapels because I don't have a lot to say to Christian kids that they haven't already heard. My pattern of a few funny jokes, a couple of tear-jerk stories, and a call for commitment is what they hear week after week.

Many kids on Christian campuses seem to feel a little second class when they compare schools. They think things just aren't as good as they are over at the big public high school. Instead of senior prom, the Christian school sponsors a senior banquet. Instead of a football team, they have a soccer team.

What bothers me the most is that there doesn't seem to be a safe place for those kids to talk about their problems. I know that not all Christian high schools are this way, but the ones I've worked with seem to perpetuate students' problems and anxieties.

Sometimes students who attend Christian schools are so protected from worldly influences that when they inevitably face the temptations that their parents and teachers feared would corrupt them, they have no idea how to respond. If they respond incorrectly to temptation, they not only feel guilty about falling short of the ideals presented by the school, but they sometimes face rejection in the form of suspension and public embarrassment for their spiritual failures.

So how do I minister to kids on Christian campuses?

Christian school kids definitely are a different breed to work with. One of the ways I've been able to break down the walls with these kids is by getting them involved with missions and service. They need to be challenged to use practically the storehouse of knowledge that they're getting at the Christian high school.

I encourage students from Christian campuses to put their faith in practice through outreach and discipleship. Things like latchkey kids' programs and mission trips seem to really ignite the students.

Second, I make sure that students from Christian campuses have my ear. I let them know I don't expect them to live perfect lives with no problems.

Finally, I try to give as much attention to the events at the Christian high school as I do to the public high school. These students need to feel that I don't think their school is second-class.

Christian School Teachers

I have great respect for teachers in Christian schools. Most are underpaid, overworked, and, in many cases, unappreciated.

Being part of the Christian school movement puts the Christian school teacher at an economic and professional disadvantage. It's wonderful to see their warm commitment to Jesus and to watch how they minister to kids.

On the other hand, there have been times when I launched a good program at my church, only to discover six months later that the local Christian high school was trying to duplicate it on the campus. Christian schools have a great advantage over us youth workers. Parents contribute money and a lot of time and support to these schools. Kids feel the pressure of pleasing their teachers and coaches as well as the desire to make good grades. Therefore, when kids have to choose between a missions trip with the high school and a trip with the church, most of them will pick the one at school.

I've also had a problem with working around the Christian high school schedule. Just when we have our best events planned, the Christian high school decides to have a special event, forcing kids to make difficult choices.

So how do I minister to teachers on Christian campuses?

Building a relationship with the administration at the Christian high school has helped my scheduling problems. More direct communication has helped reduce my sense of competition. Again, if any of these teachers or coaches attend my church, I try to build a personal relationship with them. I also try to involve them in my ministry in some way. I encourage them to get to know students from public schools, and occasionally I invite them to speak at youth group meetings.

One group of youth pastors produces a newsletter for the Christian high school, mapping out dates and key events for youth groups from all the local churches. This newsletter is sent to all the Christian high school teachers so they're aware of some of the things that are going on in the churches.

Small Church Spotlight

My church is in an unusual community. This small suburb of Chicago was originally a farming community. By the 1980s, most of the farmland had been replaced by a high-tech corridor.

Many people in the community have gone on to other blue-collar jobs, but there has been a rapid increase in the number of white-collar suburbanites moving into the community, bringing affluence.

This presents a strange environment for students. As incredible as it may seem, over the past 15 years I've worked with only three families where the parents had college educations. Few students have been career-oriented, and even fewer have been college-oriented.

Since most parents have only high school educations, their sons and daughters are content to receive high school diplomas and see no need for further education. Yet they live in a highly affluent community where advanced degrees are required for even average-paying jobs.

Just as teachers find it difficult to motivate students to think ambitiously about their futures, I find it difficult to motivate students to more mature levels of spirituality. Many seem to be satisfied with making an initial decision for Christ without pursuing how to live a Christlike life.

I've found that encouraging students to be more ambitious and more goal-oriented in thinking about their vocation makes it easier to motivate them in their spiritual lives. I've done this by taking students to college fairs, making weekend visits to colleges and universities, and occasionally tutoring students. In addition, I've shared my own college and work experiences with students to help them form dreams for their futures and find ways to accomplish those dreams.

Scripture Meditation

"Whatever town or village you enter, search for some worthy person there and stay at his house until you leave. As you enter the home, give it your greeting. If the home is deserving, let your peace rest on it; if it is not, let your peace return to you. If anyone will not welcome you or listen to your words, shake the dust off your feet when you leave that home or town. I tell you the truth, it will be more bearable for Sodom and Gomorrah on the day of judgment than for that town. I am sending you out like sheep among wolves. Therefore be as shrewd as snakes and as innocent as doves" (Matthew 10:11-16).

Spend some time meditating on what God has to say to you. Use the following questions to study this passage.

1. What principle of ministry did Jesus set forth in His instructions to His disciples?

2. What does it mean to be "sheep among wolves"?

3. What "greeting" have you received from teachers, coaches, and schools where you minister? How have you responded?

4. How can you be both shrewd and innocent as you deal with your community?

Father, help me to be a wise peacemaker in my community.

CHURCH STAFF AND CONGREGATION

You and Your Church Staff and Congregation

	Strongly Disagree	Disagree	Somewhat Disagree	Undecided	Agree	Somewhat Agree	Strongly Agree
I have enough staff/volunteers for each of my current programs.	12	18	19	1	14	27	9
It's hard to recruit enough volunteers at my church.	5	15	25	5	15	21	13
Our youth group members feel like an integral part of our church.	4	8	11	12	34	22	9
Our church members genuinely know and love the people in the youth group.	1	11	8	11	29	32	8
I conduct (or provide) regular training sessions for all staff members.	4	15	9	16	19	24	13
I try to work competent young people into leadership roles in their own programs.	3	3	3	8	19	40	24
I have a good relationship with the church staff (senior pastor, secretary, etc.).	0	0	1	3	7	36	53
I often have to justify youth activities to church members or committees.	19	36	15	3	15	5	7

Figures have been rounded to the nearest whole percentage.

Summary

Most youth workers (96%) feel they have good relationships with the church staff. Only 1% felt their relationship with the staff was questionable. Volunteer staffing seemed to be a point of struggle for 49%, while 27% feel they have to justify youth activities to the church staff and congregation.

In this chapter, Ridge shares the importance of gaining support from the church staff and congregation. As you check out our advice and comments, ask yourself:

➤ How would others rate my relationship with various members of the church staff?

➤ Do I have the full support of my church congregation? Why or why not?

➤ What can I do to improve my relationship with the senior pastor?

Youth Workers Speak:

"I don't like being misunderstood by church leaders. I get frustrated with older adults who don't understand youth ministry and throw a wet blanket on the difficult process of leading today's youth to the Lord."

Conflict between a youth pastor and a church staff or congregation is not unusual. Sometimes youth leaders are perceived as young, reckless individuals who do wild and crazy things with teenagers—namely things that are messy and expensive (two things adults do not like!).

Part of youth ministry is marketing. We need to promote youth ministry in the church body. Some of us do this naturally. I enjoy talking to people about what I'm doing with students. Others have to lobby very intentionally to gain support from the church staff and congregation.

Custodians

Our church had just completed its new $5 million building, complete with a revolving door and a brand new gym. Our staff was so excited to finally have the space for ministry after about three years of makeshift facilities at schools and homes.

An alarm system had been installed to prevent theft. However, it also prevented anybody from entering the building during odd hours. Not long after the alarm system was installed, I set off the alarm for the first time.

We had just come back from a long winter retreat. With the delays of snow and ice, flat tires, and bathroom stops, our buses arrived late enough that the alarm system was already on for the evening. My only choice was to set it off. When the police came, we explained what had happened, and they were quite kind. But I was not prepared for the custodian's response. Besides calling me insensitive and having no respect for my authority, he called me a jerk and wanted to know why I thought I could break the rules whenever I wanted to.

"What was I supposed to do?" I asked him. "The kids needed to make phone calls to their parents so they could pick them up.

Where were they supposed to go to the bathroom? Were we supposed to stand outside in the cold?"

I remember the heated discussions that took place in the staff meetings in the following weeks as we talked about the custodial work and how the janitor felt abused by the pastoral staff.

The custodian/youth pastor relationship is a difficult one. My job is to use the building to its utmost capacity while the custodian's job is to maintain the facilities. Therefore, it's not unusual for me to be in conflict with the church custodian.

So how do I relate effectively with the church custodian?

During my ministry, I have learned some things that have helped my relationships with the custodians.

First, I want to win the custodial staff over to the goals and objectives of my youth ministry. Even though some of our skits and games may create some problems for the custodians, I want them to understand that we're on the same team, changing lives for Christ. So I might invite them to an event or ask them to help me with one particular project where they actually participate in the program.

Second, I challenge the custodian to recognize that his or her job is one of being a servant to the body of Christ, and that sometimes includes those junior high kids that mess up the bathrooms time after time. I'm not talking about kids who damage the building, but rather normal wear and tear. Any time you get a group of kids in a room, there's going to be some mud on the carpet, walls scraped by chairs, or food dropped on the floor. So I challenge the custodial staff to look at themselves as servants in addition to being caretakers of the buildings. Many times it seems that custodians lose track of the fact that they are employed to support the staff, not to preserve the building.

Third, I try to communicate on a regular basis with the custodian. I've found that my ability to get along with the custodian is almost directly in proportion to how much time I spend communicating with him or her. I do this by giving the custodian my youth calendar and describing the events that will take place and what rooms will be used. In this way, the custodian can feel that I am working alongside him or her.

Secretaries

I've never had very good relationships with my secretaries. We didn't have major fights, but they've never been the best part of my team relationships. Most of the blame can be placed on me.

First of all, I was never taught how to work with a secretary. There were no classes in seminary or Bible school that helped me understand what secretaries do and how they can make my job easier. Therefore, I learned by trial and error.

Betty was my absolute favorite secretary. She was the church secretary for the pastor, the Christian Education director, and me in my very first church. She was an older woman who really liked kids, and therefore she liked me. What I appreciated about Betty was that she took the time to help me organize my job and understand what I was doing that made her job more difficult. Betty and I certainly had conflicts, but we also had a cooperative spirit which made my ministry more effective.

So how can I have a healthy relationship with the church secretary?

First, I try to never give my secretary instructions as I'm running by his or her desk. I have a terrible tendency to run off to meet a kid for an appointment and on my way by the secretary's desk, say, "You need to call this person to do this and this." Then I'm gone before he or she has time to respond or figure out what I want done.

Another thing I've done to create a better relationship is to invite the secretary into my office and pass on the information directly. If I write down and organize what I want to be done, the secretary usually feels that I've thought through what I'm asking him or her to do. The secretary knows exactly what's expected and can ask me questions about things he or she may not fully understand.

Finally, I try to include my secretary in some youth events. For instance, I might invite the person to come on a retreat or attend an event where he or she can see the fruits of our labor.

Associate Staff

A certain amount of sibling rivalry goes on in multiple-staff situations where there's a senior pastor, music pastor, Christian Education pastor, visitation pastor, or maybe another pastor within the youth department (college or junior high). During my ministry, my rivalries have not been with the senior pastor, but with the associate staff.

At one church, I developed a very close relationship with the senior pastor. But that friendship seemed to create some jealousy and hard feelings among the associate staff and vice versa. I found myself having to work at being excited about another staff member's successes. This does not make for great staff relationships.

The way I boasted about my ministry, how much money I had in my budget, how much information I knew about the church that another staff member didn't know, and what meetings I was invited to all influenced the way other staff members perceived me—and it fostered rivalry.

So how can I have better staff relationships?

I've learned some things about ministering as a team and avoiding staff rivalry. First of all, information in church work is powerful. When I know information that other staff members don't know, tension and irritation grows. So I try to share information with other staff people. As the church struggles with different problems and strives to reach its goals, and as I move up the organizational ladder, I need to share whatever information "power" I have with the associate staff.

Second, the most important consideration in my staff relationships is my friendship with the senior pastor. I have had three great senior pastors who have become very close friends. But that friendship sometimes gets in the way of ministering together. When one staff member has a more intimate relationship with the senior pastor than other staff members, the remaining staff sometimes feels that person has more authority and influence in the church. They become even more sensitive to what they perceive as favoritism as they try to get resources to accomplish their ministries. I try to avoid creating jealousy by making sure that I keep my friendship-building times with the senior pastor separate from work.

Third, I have developed better relationships with the staff by using them in my ministry to speak at a retreat or substitute teach for me. Occasionally I ask a staff member to participate in a parents' meeting or on a panel.

Fourth, I try to affirm and care for other staff members. When they miss events or are late for meetings, I avoid pointing out their weaknesses. When they make positive steps in their ministries, I try to encourage them in a creative way.

Senior Pastor

At the three churches where I have served, the senior pastors have become my best friends during that period of ministry. I found that they not only had a ministry to me, but that I had a ministry to them. They were the kind of people with whom I could share not just ideas for ministry, but also my personal life and problems.

In general, I believe that a youth ministry is only as strong as the ministry of the senior pastor. It's very difficult to sustain a youth ministry when the senior pastor's leadership is weak or indifferent. There are always exceptions, but the senior pastor sets a tone by either encouraging creative youth ministry or restricting it.

I would go on to say that a youth ministry is very dependent on what happens on Sunday mornings. We need to find ways to integrate students into the morning worship service. The better the relationship the senior pastor has with students, the more he influences those students' understanding of the church and Christ's relationship to them.

So how do I relate to the senior pastor?

As an associate staff member, I first remind myself that the senior pastor is my boss. He has the responsibility and power to shape my ministry, and my job is to magnify my boss's strengths and minimize his weaknesses.

The second ingredient for a good relationship with the senior pastor is to realize that most senior pastors are lonely. There are very few people in the church with whom they can share openly and with confidence. At the same time, there are only a few people outside the church with whom they can express their feelings about the members of the church and how their ministry is going. Many times the only confidant they can find is a person on staff. One thing I can do for the senior pastor is work on becoming a good friend.

I also should allow the senior pastor to be a discipler in my life. He should be showing me how ministry should be done. Building a relationship with the senior pastor allows me to ask him questions about his methods and approaches to accomplishing ministry.

Staff Meetings

One of the problems with staff meetings is that 90% of what goes on in them does not pertain directly to *my* ministry. I don't find it very exciting or entertaining to be talking about the nursery, college ministry, senior citizens' ministry, or even the format of the morning worship service. And yet I have a double standard toward staff meetings. I definitely want others' undivided attention and involvement whenever I try to make decisions about my ministry.

Part of me wants to participate in the decisions made in staff meetings. In my experience, though, it seems that the changes discussed in staff meetings rarely get put into practice. Therefore, most staff meetings are either very frustrating or very stressful for me.

The staff at one of my churches was particularly difficult to work with. First of all, there were 12 of us in the staff meeting. Those 12 had at least six different perspectives. One person always confronted a problem from a spiritual standpoint: "We need to pray for an answer to this problem." Another person tackled the same problem from a marketing standpoint: "If church members knew what was going on, they would give more." Another person represented a pastoral concern: "People don't feel cared for." This dynamic created a real grind at the meetings. I found myself unmotivated and didn't put much into these gatherings compared to what many of the others were doing.

At one church where I served, the pastoral staff did not function as a team. There was a lot of competition, anger, and talking about each other outside of staff meetings. Some staff members came with every intention of dominating staff meetings with their agendas. Other staff members wouldn't participate because they knew their suggestions would be misinterpreted. Then there were people who wanted business as usual and tried to rescue the situation by smoothing out ruffled feathers. To put it mildly, staff meetings in that church were not fun.

Yet at another church, staff meetings were just delightful. We'd eat lunch together, spend time fellowshipping and praying together, and then work out our own agenda. We accomplished a great deal.

So how do I participate more effectively in staff meetings?

Even though staff meetings aren't always important to me, they are important to others. I have five rules for staff meetings.

First, I try to ask questions instead of making statements at staff meetings. To keep my interest up, I ask questions about why things are being done and how I can help. I try to show interest by questioning other staff members rather than giving my uninformed opinion.

Second, I prepare for staff meetings. When I'm asked to present something to the rest of the staff, I prepare for that staff meeting as if I were getting ready for a parents' meeting. I make sure my proposals are in writing, and I encourage questions so they know I really want their input. I try to use staff meetings as a forum for new ideas. I recognize that the staff represents portions of the congregation, and I need to know how they will respond to ideas for my ministry.

Third, I try to keep silent in staff meetings. I love to talk about other areas of the church, and sometimes I meddle in things that are not in my realm of influence. Therefore, I try to be quiet about things I don't really need to have an opinion about. Sometimes giving an opinion off the top of my head can do great damage to my relationship with other staff members.

Fourth, I view staff meetings as an easy way to give support to the rest of the staff. I try to maintain regular attendance at these meetings. In the past I found myself making every excuse possible to miss staff meetings. In fact, there were times when I would purposely schedule a counseling appointment with a kid at the same time as a staff meeting so I would have an excuse not to go. The message I was sending to the rest of the staff was that their needs were not important to me. By simply investing one or two hours in the staff meeting each week, and being as energetic and enthusiastic as possible about that time together, I can show great support for our team.

Once I brought a bunch of thank-you letters that I needed to write to a staff meeting because I knew I was going to be bored. Halfway through the meeting the executive pastor stopped and said, "Ridge, I know that we all have work to do, and we're all concerned about what takes place. However, I'm going to ask you not to write those letters during this meeting because we're interpreting that as your lack of interest in what we're about."

He was right. That's what I was demonstrating. And I thanked him for calling me on that. I keep in mind now that staff meetings can be the easiest time for us to show support for each other.

Finally, I make staff meetings a priority in my week. I don't show up late or leave early. I stay for the entire meeting. In fact, I schedule a buffer of time so that if the meeting runs long, I don't have to get up and leave.

Church Politics

One of the churches where I have ministered calls itself a quiet charismatic church. It believes in all the gifts of the Holy Spirit, but the more controversial gifts of healing and speaking in tongues are not practiced in the morning worship service. However, these gifts may be practiced in some of the small group ministries of the church.

The more expressive people attending that church wanted it to become more charismatic. A large group with roots in mainline denominations wanted it to be charismatic enough to make it lively and energetic, but not charismatic enough to make anyone uncomfortable. This stance created an interesting church polity. Thus, choosing board members or inviting someone to speak took on political as well as spiritual repercussions.

I have a tendency sometimes to get involved with church politics. I have a basic desire to be in the know and in control. Even though I'm not a good meeting person, I like to be invited to meetings in case an issue comes up where I want to offer input. When I'm not invited to the elders' meetings, I'm always wondering what the elders are thinking and doing. It's very easy for me to resort to manipulation and maneuvering to make sure my issues get heard and to produce the responses I want.

Youth ministry is sometimes directly affected by politics in the church. One of my ministries was in a community where several Sunday School curriculum publishers are located. Since our church was the largest in town, it became a political issue to determine which Sunday School curriculum we should use. The publishers didn't put pressure on us, but some of their employees had influence in the church. I suspect the issue became not what curriculum was best for our students, but which publisher would get our business.

I didn't want to use any Sunday School curriculum. My staff was small, and the church's facilities prevented me from breaking my 80 students into the small groups that the curriculum was designed for. I soon became unpopular with some of those influential people because I wasn't using Sunday School curriculum.

So how do I deal with church politics?

I need to recognize that all church work is going to involve politics to some extent, but my job is bring factions together into the body of Christ. A very practical way to do that is by being a good listener. Sometimes "political" people just want to be heard; they don't necessarily need to have action taken on the issues they're raising. So it's very important that I provide them with forums where they can express themselves. In youth ministry those forums are parents' meetings for high school and junior high school ministries. The more people feel we are listening, and the more we do in fact listen to people, the less political the church will become.

At one church we had a Christian school that rented our building during the week. As the church grew, we needed to ask that school to leave so that the church would have room to expand. It became very awkward, as there was a lot of emotional energy attached to this issue. I planned a meeting for the parents and the concerned people of our church simply to listen to one another about the issues. It didn't become a gripe session or a platform to gain more support. Listening diffused a lot of the emotion.

There are some other things I've learned about why *I* get drawn into church politics. First, I want to be accountable for my ministry. I don't just want the duties and responsibilities of youth work without the authority to make important decisions for my ministry. So if I sense I'm losing that control or authority to others, I tend to become defensive and concerned that things go my way. But when I go beyond concern and become manipulative and overtly political, I'm probably overlooking the fact that I need to be submissive to the people to whom God has called me.

Therefore I've realized that it's better that I'm not invited to some decision-making meetings because it forces me to acknowledge the fact that I'm under the authority of others. And second, some church business is really none of my business. I do not need to know about everything that is done at the church.

Church Committees

Church boards and committees scare me because they hold so much power. When they meet, I always wonder what kinds of things they are talking about and how their decisions will influence my ministry. They intimidate me.

Too often I feel manipulated by committees. Many times I wish I reported only to the senior pastor or the elders. But in my experience, I have been accountable to the youth commission, the Christian Education board, and the missions committee.

When I go to a board meeting, I am not always sure how to communicate with the members. Even the way boardrooms are set up kind of scares me. All of the chairs, chalkboards, charts, and big piles of paper that seem to fill the room can make a person feel very small.

Church boards and committees sometimes make me angry because they make decisions and set policies in areas that they don't seem to know too much about. It's often difficult to give the church board enough information and data so they can make informed decisions. I'm not sure most board members really understand what curriculum should be taught in the eighth-grade Sunday School class, and yet many church boards feel qualified to make that choice.

So how do I relate to church boards and committees?

I've come to realize that committees are an important part of church work and that I need to treat them as such. Therefore, when I go to a committee or board meeting, I try to anticipate all the questions and comments that they might have about my area of ministry.

I've also realized that church committees are composed of volunteers. Committee members are sacrificing their time for an extracurricular activity. They come to meetings with their minds still focused on work, the stock market, their children, their spouses, and so forth. Part of their inability to get things done expediently is sometimes due to distractions.

Because these people don't have a lot of time, they sometimes express themselves more strongly than what they really feel.

They want to make sure that they say things as forcefully as possible in the least amount of time. That scares me a little bit. But I can overcome that fear if I can identify the presuppositions, backgrounds, and assumptions of various committee members.

I try to provide committees with written information about the decisions I want them to make *before* they come to meetings. This way they have time to digest the material without feeling rushed to make decisions.

Uninformed Church Members

Uninformed church members are usually present at business meetings and parents' meetings. They also express themselves in letters to the board. These people have just enough information to make them dangerous. You know, the church member who stands up at the church business meeting and makes an impassioned plea for our kids to be educated in the Word of God because the youth pastor isn't really leading appropriate Bible study. Of course that person hasn't read the page of the youth ministry report that talks about small group discipleship and the curriculum I'm using. This member probably heard from one person—perhaps a kid who has left the youth group—that we never study the Bible.

So how do I relate to uninformed church members?

I've learned that critics fill a vacuum. In other words, if there is a quiet time at a meeting, or if there's an opportunity for questions and answers to be entertained, critics with agendas will stand up and try to fill that dead air. Recognizing that fact, I try to include appropriate information about what the youth are doing in a monthly newsletter, in Sunday bulletins, and in the annual report of the church.

I've also realized that people have a right to ask any questions. They should know what's going on in the church and in my ministry. If church members don't know about youth events, it's probably because I haven't given them the proper tools and information. My job is to inform these people before they get into a place where they can do damage, such as a business meeting or a parents' meeting. When I communicate with these members, they usually provide me with an avenue of acceptance, not an attitude of criticism.

Another way I help uninformed church members is to make sure I keep regular office hours. Concerned church members, as well as parents and staff, know they can contact me on certain days between certain hours. This practice can work well with both paid church staff and volunteers.

Informed Church Members

What really ticks me off in ministry are people who *do* know what's going on in my ministry yet fail to offer verbal support. Occasionally, I face (usually alone) challenges to my ministry, and people who know about the activities of my youth group do not seem to want to help. I've found that people who are satisfied with my performance don't want to say anything. They like what's going on but don't realize that I need help.

For example, I had a social at one kid's house whose parents spent a lot of time with the youth group. But when questions were raised in a parents' meeting about my effectiveness in meeting students' social needs, instead of sharing with the other parents, this couple remained quiet. These parents who had extended their hospitality seemed to say, "OK, Ridge, it's your show. Hope you can give the right answers."

In contrast, at another church, a printer whose two children were involved in my youth group was extremely supportive of my ministry. Occasionally I would have Art talk to another member of the church to share what was really going on in the youth work. Art did a lot of printing for me for free or at a reduced price. Many times I was accused of spending too much money on flyers and brochures. Art was very good at informing people about the facts.

So how do I encourage informed members to visibly support my ministry?

One of the ways I've helped informed church members to vocalize their support is by appointing certain individuals to be spokespeople at various church meetings. I ask them to give their testimony about what's happening in their family and in the lives of their kids. My goal is to help the church get a handle on the value of my ministry.

I remember the day that Jim's mom stood up at a parents meeting and told how one of my youth staff had gone over to her house and prayed with Jim before a major soccer game. What she communicated about how my ministry was dedicated to caring about each kid individually and the necessity of having appropriate staff to do such ministry was far more effective than anything I could have said. Informed, supportive parents and volunteers can be the spokespersons who help us get the enthusiastic support and care our ministries need.

Small Church Spotlight

In a small church like mine, with only one or two people on staff, size limits support but lessens the distance between staff members and congregation. Unfortunately, smaller churches do not necessarily make for better communication.

My biggest frustration is with uninformed church members. At quarterly congregational meetings, I repeatedly hear this comment: "I don't know what you're doing with the youth. How come you never tell us what you're doing?"

As a part-time youth worker, I naturally don't have time to put out weekly or even monthly reports on youth events. However, activities other than regular meetings are usually announced from the pulpit on Sunday mornings.

Though the volunteers who work with me usually share information with other church members and support me at these meetings, I always feel as if these uninformed individuals don't trust me. I've encouraged them to visit our youth programs, or to ask me what we're studying in Sunday School or what our retreat theme will be, but the complainers have not taken me up on these suggestions.

I've learned to respond to these individuals by listening with a calm heart. I try to remember that such people are only one or two voices of the church—and usually they're not parents. When I put their complaints in perspective, I realize that I have quite a bit of pastoral and congregational support for my ministry. And over the years, I've found that I can weather complaints if I have pastoral support, but I stand alone without it.

Scripture Meditation

"It was he who gave some to be apostles, some to be prophets, some to be evangelists, and some to be pastors and teachers, to prepare God's people for works of service, so that the body of Christ may be built up until we all reach unity in the faith and in the knowledge of the Son of God and become mature, attaining to the whole measure of the fullness of Christ. . . .

"From him the whole body, joined and held together by every supporting ligament, grows and builds itself up in love, as each part does its work" (Ephesians 4:11-13, 16).

Spend some time meditating on what God has to say to you. Use the following questions to study this passage.

1. Why do you think Paul mentioned the callings of apostles, prophets, evangelists, and so on in this passage?

2. What is the purpose of having people with all these gifts?

3. In what ways do you need to "join and hold together" with other staff members? With church members?

4. Has an unhealthy relationship between you and another staff member prevented your youth group from being built up?

5. What can you do to encourage other staff members and individual members of the congregation to exercise their gifts?

Father, help me to contribute to the growth and building up of my church staff and congregation.

PARENTS

You and Parents

	Strongly Disagree	Disagree	Somewhat Disagree	Undecided	Agree	Somewhat Agree	Strongly Agree
I get a lot of support from my youth members' parents.	4	4	7	3	30	31	13
Parents are involved in our activities on a regular basis.	7	19	17	4	24	23	6
I meet with each youth group member's parent(s) at least once a year.	8	11	12	12	15	33	9
I suspect abuse (physical, sexual, etc.) in the homes of some of my students.	13	19	8	12	19	23	6
Parents should take more responsibility for the spiritual development of their children.	0	0	1	1	6	31	61

Figures have been rounded to the nearest whole percentage.

Summary

Among those youth workers surveyed, there seems to be disparity in the amount of parental involvement in youth work. Approximately 53% agreed that parents were involved on a regular basis while 43% felt that parents weren't very involved in their youth programs. Given the fact that only 1 in 10 parents think it's important for their children to be involved in religious activities, developing a relationship with youth workers and supporting their programs may not be a priority for many families.[3]

In this chapter, Ridge shares the struggles and challenges of working with parents—good, bad, and hurting ones. As you check out our advice and comments, ask yourself:

➤ How can I gain more support from my students' parents?

➤ How am I showing parents that I care about them?

➤ Do I have the courage to challenge parents who are hurting their children by leading damaging lifestyles?

Youth Workers Speak:

"It hurts when a parent resists letting his or her child know the Lord. I get frustrated with parents who don't live like Christians when they claim to be just that."

A few years ago our church hired a consultant. This well-known consultant spent half a day with each of the six pastors on our staff. During my time with him, we went for a long walk on the beach. He only asked me one question.

"Ridge, who would you say were your top 10 students in 15 years of youth ministry? Which students would reach the Ridge Burns' Youth Ministry Hall of Fame?"

For the next two hours I told him great stories of 10 students whom I really loved, respected, and viewed as the fruit of my ministry. When I got through with the long, detailed descriptions of those kids, the consultant responded.

"Ridge, let me make two observations about the disciples you say are the result of your youth ministry. The first observation is that those students were all high achievers. They did some great things for God, and you motivated them to do those things.

"The second observation is that all 10 of these students had the support of Mom or Dad. They had one parent who really supported them and was their cheerleader."

This consultant went on to say that perhaps I was taking the credit for the work of good families, and maybe the best way to disciple kids today is to help provide them with a good environment at home where they can be effectively discipled. In fact, the consultant felt that half of youth ministry needs to include working with parents, a trend he thinks will be the wave of the future.

I've learned some things about parents since I've become one. I've learned the three Cs of working with parents. First, we need to *care* for parents. There are parents who really look to us for care, support, and encouragement, so part of our ministry needs to be in tune with them.

The second C is that we need to invite parents to *come* to youth programs and events. Instead of looking at parents as enemies, we need to look at them as people who want to understand what we're doing.

Finally we need to *challenge* parents. In my ministry on the West Coast, I've learned of parents who actually provide their kids with narcotics. It's amazing that some parents do not recognize the impact of their lifestyles on their kids. When I am in the pulpit, in parents' meetings, or talking one-on-one, I try to take advantage of these opportunities to challenge parents about their own lifestyles and what they're doing to their kids.

Good Parents

When I think back on my years of ministry, the best parents I've ever known were Larry and Naomi. They had two sons and an adopted Korean daughter. As my wife, Robanne, and I watched how they managed their family and showed respect for one another, we knew we wanted to follow their model in our own parenting.

Larry and Naomi were good parents for several reasons. They listened well not just to each other, but also to their kids. They respected their kids, but they were firm disciplinarians when necessary.

I always know when a student has good parents, even if I've never met Mom and Dad. The student usually has a reasonable amount of self-esteem, knows how to express affection, and isn't embarrassed to discuss his or her family.

So how do I deal with good parents?

Having good parents around creates some interesting dynamics for a youth group. Do I use the parents as youth sponsors? How do they relate to their kids? Do they intimidate other parents who may not be as effective as they are?

In my relationship with Larry and Naomi, I learned three

things about working with good parents. First, I want to use good parents as personal advisors. For example, I would call Larry and Naomi and share with them in an anonymous way some of the problems I was facing with students. I was able to get advice from a parent's perspective. They were confidential and very supportive.

Second, I use good parents to help other parents. I remember one situation where a couple was having problems with their son obeying a curfew. I suggested that they give Larry and Naomi a call to find out how they handled that problem with their sons. Having the parents exchange ideas was far more powerful than me giving advice as a nonparent.

Third, I ask them to pray for and support the other parents of my students. Larry and Naomi had a sensitivity to parents who were hurting, so they formed a parents' support group. Even though *they* weren't necessarily hurting, they knew how much their kids meant to them and wanted other parents to know they had a place to share their concerns for their children.

Hurting Parents

Leanne was a phenomenal girl. She was blond and popular, and she seemed to love the Lord. Her family was wonderful, supportive, and caring, and they spent time listening to her. But Leanne was addicted to alcohol. Her parents had no idea that she was an alcoholic or that she was suffering with depression, which forced her to drink. When I sat across the table from Leanne's parents and looked into their faces, I found myself in tears as I recommended they put their daughter in a treatment center for adolescent alcoholics.

The question becomes: *How do I know when a parent is hurting?* The question becomes even more complicated when dealing with parents like Leanne's, who seem confident and have reached a certain degree of success. What clues helped me to sense that Leanne's parents were hurting?

First, Leanne's parents told me they were hurting. Sometimes parents are at the end of their rope. Parents who call me in the middle of the night or early in the morning to tell me about problems with their kids are hurting.

Second, as Leanne's problems began to surface, her parents began to withdraw. They had been very active participants in our church, so I took my clue from their change of behavior. When parents are hurting, their behavior sometimes changes in a very dramatic way.

Another clue that parents are hurting is their sudden disenchantment with the pastoral staff, the musicians, or even the youth pastor. When parents who have been really supportive suddenly become very vocal about the need for change in the church, we may want to step back and see if these parents are hurting.

Finally, I knew Leanne's parents were hurting because I really believe God revealed their pain to me. As we pray and think about the families who are in our charge, God will reveal the needs of hurting parents.

So how can I help hurting parents?

Parents can be terribly hurt by their children, and somehow, we as youth workers need to come to grips with how we can help parents be more effective. First, we need to realize that parents who are hurting are desperate. I know this because of my own difficulties in parenting my five-year-old. Because this is my first experience as a father, I'm desperately seeking new, vital information about kids. When parents are desperate, we can provide them with books, counseling referrals, information on substance abuse programs and support groups, and contact with other parents who are experiencing some of the same hurts.

In fact, one of the best ways I've found to help hurting parents is to get them talking to each other. They will discover then that they're not alone in their pain. Sometimes I schedule parent meetings that include a short problem-sharing time at the beginning. I tell the parents that this is an opportunity for them to talk with each other about common problems with their kids.

Around the meeting area I arrange signs with the words *curfew, drugs, academic performance, authority, household chores, time management,* and *other youth problems.* At each one of those signs, I ask a parent of a student who has struggled with their child in that area to be a facilitator for discussion. I ask the rest of the parents in the room to go to one of the signs that describes the problem they would like to talk about regarding their own children.

After about 20 minutes, parents can go to another sign. This way parents get to listen to other parents who have similar problems. These mothers and fathers start to feel like they are not alone. They can also share ideas about ways to solve problems.

The second way I help hurting parents is by listening to them. If I have open office hours, parents can drop in or make an appointment. I have even scheduled open houses after church in our home where parents who are hurting can come and talk and pray about their kids.

Finally, we need to pray *for* and *with* the parents of our students, not just look at them as enemies or people we have to get along with because we feel obligated to. We need to pray *with* them that God would really use them to disciple their kids.

Bad Parents

I hate working with students who have bad parents. Don't get me wrong—I don't hate the students—I hate the fact that there are no requirements for the job of parenthood.

In the same way that I know which students have good parents, I can recognize students who have bad parents. These students usually have low self-images, withhold affection, and never mention their families. These students usually have no curfews, exhibit little discretion about their appearances, and have numerous problems in their school, social, and spiritual lives.

Roger's parents are terrible parents. They don't care about where he goes, if he graduates from school, if he drinks, smokes pot, has sex with his girlfriend, and so on. They would like to be rid of Roger. Their unwillingness to spend time with Roger amounts to doing just that. Throwing him away. They feel burdened by Roger. And I'm finding more and more parents who are just plain bad parents because they're too selfish.

So how do I counteract the effects of bad parents?

First, I work hard to support kids who have terrible parents. I need to spend lots of time with them. And it's important that the time we spend with these kids is not spent griping about the parents. These kids need some form of support structure other than the questionable friends they hang out with at school. Roger and I got together regularly. It took time, effort, and scheduling on my part, but I knew nobody else was listening to Roger.

Second, I offer suggestions to these kids with bad parents on how to get help. If the parents are abusive, I give students hot line numbers and information on agencies that provide advocates for abused family members. I also create support groups. Even if it's only in groups of three or four kids in a Sunday School class, there is usually more than one kid in a small group who has parents who are struggling.

Third, I try to recognize my limitations in helping people like Roger. There is very little I can do to provide the right kind of home environment for Roger. And when I confront Roger, his parents don't support my confrontations, so he takes the line of least resistance. So I need to admit that I may be powerless to help some kids whose home lives are suffering.

Parents with Agendas

I've always struggled with how to get a music program in a church moving in the same direction as a growing high school or junior high school program. At one church, I had a wonderful, strong youth program. Kids were involved in missions, evangelism, and discipleship groups, but there were several parents who felt we needed a high school choir. They made it very clear to the church board that there was something lacking because I didn't have a high school choir.

The church only had a part-time music pastor, so the board decided to bring on a full-time music pastor to organize a complete choir system arranged by school grades. Of course, the first choir he wanted to start was the high school choir. So he asked the kids to come to practice on Sunday afternoons. Quite a few kids showed up the first time. But over the year, the numbers began to dwindle, and pretty soon the high school choir became the youth choir, combining junior highers with high schoolers. And with a youth group that numbered close to 300 students (junior high and high school), less than thirty were participating in the youth choir.

I could have told the board and the music pastor that it wouldn't work. I knew the kids were overcommitted and most weren't really interested in music anyway. I couldn't even get them to sing on retreats. In addition, the music programs in the high schools were so much superior to the music program in the church that the few who really enjoyed singing were involved in school programs and felt no need to join the youth choir.

So how can I deal with parents who have agendas?

I can't figure out parents who have agendas. I can't reason with parents who feel that the needs of their own kids are more important than the agenda of the entire youth group. Therefore, I've learned first of all to define where I am going so that the parents with agendas can react to my goals and objectives. If they know what's going on, they cannot protest that there's a vacuum within my ministry.

Second, I make no promises to parents with agendas. Sometimes I have a great desire to do whatever they want because it will get them off my back and stop their harassment. If I make promises, my youth program becomes filled with things parents have encouraged me to do, but not necessarily what I feel God has called me to do.

Finally, I try to listen to the parents with agendas. Sometimes they just need to express what they're feeling and don't really need me to respond or take action. Sometimes parents with agendas are right in their perceptions. Sometimes they are pointing out weaknesses in my program where I need to make some changes.

Parents' Meetings

When I first came to one of my churches, I called every student on the mailing list, except for a few I couldn't reach. The few students I couldn't reach felt slighted. One student's feelings were especially wounded. His parents came fuming to a parents' meeting, feeling as if I had neglected their son. When I got over my defensiveness, I realized that my lack of communication had festered in this family and had prevented me from ministering to them.

I've never been real excited about parents' meetings. In fact, they scare me. I approach them with great fear—fear that the meeting will turn hostile, fear that the parents' limited perspective of youth ministry will cause them to say things that could damage my ability to be effective in ministry, fear that the chinks in my ministry will be exposed, fear that an issue will come up where I don't have an answer, so I come off looking incompetent.

I am guilty of using four smoke screens in parents' meetings. The first smoke screen is the filibuster. I try to talk as much as possible, giving parents so much information that they can't get a word in edgewise. Second, I exploit my humor to keep parents laughing, thereby avoiding conflict. Third, if I have to discuss a controversial area, I start at a point where I feel safe and comfortable. That way the conflicts that are stressful to me are never touched. Finally, I try to evoke sympathy by confessing to the parents how I'm trying to do the best I can. Because I admit my weaknesses, parents are moved emotionally toward supporting me. These smoke screens work for a while, but in the end I've discovered that they don't foster communication and only postpone conflicts.

I've learned that parents' meetings are very important because they allow me to communicate *what* I'm doing and *why* I'm doing it. They also provide an opportunity for me to listen to some of the suggestions that parents may have.

So how do I manage parents' meetings?

I divide my parents' meetings into three parts. This arrangement allows me to answer most parents' questions before the actual question-and-answer session begins.

In the first segment I communicate to the parents what events are planned for the year, how much money the program is going to cost, and what events may be canceled during the year. I try to make available a six-month calendar that highlights socials and special events. Simply circulating a calendar reduces the chance of conflict.

In the second segment, I minister to the parents by bringing in a speaker, showing some sort of media presentation, or giving them some practical parenting suggestions.

In the third segment, I invite questions and comments. To my surprise, I find that when a conflict arises, I have no lack of supportive parents who defend me and my programs.

Parents Who Change Their Minds About Me

Dave was a wonderful sponsor. He was a supportive leader who had a flexible schedule, a van, everything I wanted from a youth sponsor. Dave really loved me for the first two years I was in ministry at his church. He would drop by my office to talk or call me at home, and he was very supportive at the church board meetings. But something happened, and I don't know what it was. For whatever reasons, Dave decided I wasn't the best person to be the youth pastor at the church. Suddenly, he was campaigning against me in meetings.

I found myself dealing with several emotions. First, I was really angry at Dave. I couldn't understand why he had changed his mind about me. Second, I was hurt. Even in my attempts to communicate with him to find out what the problems were, Dave was never straight with me. He never gave me direct answers. I also felt terribly in the dark, for I never knew what was going on when Dave would have meetings with the pastor or the Christian Education committee.

Third, I found myself becoming hostile toward Dave's kind, sweet daughter who was in my youth group. I began acting out my anger and hurt against her because of her father's change of behavior.

So how do I deal with parents who change their minds about me?

There are some things I've learned about working with parents whose regard for me as youth pastor changes. First, I've learned that there will always be these kinds of parents in youth ministry. There are parents who are going to love you at one time and hate you the next.

Second, I need to build bridges to those parents, either by offering them tasks within my youth program that may lead to open discussion, or by keeping the lines of communication open in another way.

Third, I need to avoid making concessions to these kinds of parents. I am easily manipulated by a person like Dave. My tendency is to give away the youth program just to keep peace in the family. I need to make sure that I am looking out for the welfare of all the students in the youth group rather than focusing on other agendas.

Parents Who Don't Like Me

At one church I served, there was one parent who never liked me. From the moment I came on board, Lee made it very clear that he wasn't happy with me. I don't know if it was the direction of my ministry or my personality that upset him. To prevent confrontation, I found myself avoiding Lee and trying to make sure his concerns were always cared for.

However, I soon realized I was being manipulated by this man. As I got to know him better, I noticed that part of the way Lee stayed in control of his family, his wife, his kids, and me was to project his dislike toward us so we would do things just to please him. Finally, I realized I needed to treat Lee like a normal person in the church, and I learned to live with the fact that he may not like me. I still tried to minister to him and his family as best I could.

So how do I handle parents who don't like me?

I try to recognize that people like Lee are part of the experience of ministry. I've learned to avoid thinking of parents like him as problems. As I began to understand who Lee was and spent some time with him, I began to see that he had some deep personal conflicts. His criticism of me was pretty much a smoke screen that protected him from having to reveal his own problems and deal with his own hurts. Parents like Lee are not fun to manage, but if I treat them as people, I can survive.

Parents with Youth Ministry Experience

In my opinion, these are the most troublesome kind of parents. Former youth pastors, former Christian Education majors, and people who work in Christian organizations all have just enough knowledge about youth ministry to cause problems. They are able to talk the lingo and sway committees to consider different approaches to youth ministry. And yet they may not know the kids in their own youth program. They also have a tendency to view the whole youth program as a way of serving the needs and desires of their own kids.

Sometimes these parents have knowledge of youth ministry, but they don't take into account the personal, day-to-day relationships that are a necessary part of ministry. They know what to do, but they don't spend any time with students. Ann was one such person. She was a good sponsor, but she was always quoting resources and reading books, and I felt very threatened by her knowledge.

So how do I deal with parents who have ministry experience?

Often we need to change our attitudes toward parents who have ministry experience. I began to use Ann in tough situations that only a skilled youth worker could handle. I put her in situations where she could really excel. When I used Ann effectively, *I* felt less threatened by her, and *she* felt less competitive toward me.

Parents with ministry experience may have some good advice

that may be well taken, but those parents should in turn respect my philosophy of youth ministry. Therefore, I provide parents with a written philosophy of youth ministry. That way they can take their suggestions and their comments and see where they fit in with my principles and philosophy of education. In Ann's case, some of her suggestions were wonderful additions to the youth program, and I adopted them into my philosophy.

Small Church Spotlight

Since most of the kids I work with are unchurched, I don't have close relationships with their parents. While I don't have many conflicts with those parents, I don't get much support or affirmation either. They don't attend parents' meetings, they don't fund the youth program, and they don't encourage their kids to participate.

During the past few years, I have worked very deliberately to develop better relationships with these parents. I've done this a couple of ways. One way was by raising my visibility at common, nonthreatening places such as sports events and plays. Some parents seemed more comfortable talking to me in those settings.

I have also been able to connect with some parents who have introduced me to other parents I had never met before. I began to offer to help parents run the concession stands at wrestling matches and serve as a temporary legal guardian for athletes when their parents couldn't be present at sports matches.

Another way I've developed better relationships is by asking those unchurched parents to serve as sponsors for a retreat or summer trip. Not only did it give me a chance to get to know them better, it gave them an opportunity to see what my ministry is all about.

Scripture Meditation

"Son of man, speak to your countrymen and say to them: 'When I bring the sword against a land, and the people of the land choose one of their men and make him their watchman, and he sees the sword coming against the land and blows the trumpet to warn the people, then if anyone hears the trumpet but does not take warning and the sword comes and takes his life, his blood will be on his own head. . . .

"But if the watchman sees the sword coming and does not blow the trumpet to warn the people and the sword comes and takes the life of one of them, that man will be taken away because of his sin, but I will hold the watchman accountable for his blood.

"Son of man, I have made you a watchman for the house of Israel; so hear the word I speak and give them warning from me. . . . But if you do warn the wicked man to turn from his ways and he does not do so, he will die for his sin, but you will have saved yourself" (Ezekiel 33:2-4, 6-7, 9).

97

Spend some time meditating on what God has to say to you. Use the following questions to study this passage.

1. In what ways did the prophets serve as watchmen for the people of Israel?

2. What do you learn about accountablility from this passage?

3. In what ways are you a watchman for God? Do your students' parents view you as a watchman? Why or why not?

4. What "swords" or dangers do you see approaching your students? Do you have the courage to give warnings or "blow the trumpet" for parents to hear?

5. When parents ignore your warnings, how will you respond?

Father, help me to be a spiritual watchman for my students and their parents.

CHAPTER 5

PERSONAL ISSUES

You and Personal Issues

	Strongly Disagree	Disagree	Somewhat Disagree	Undecided	Agree	Somewhat Agree	Strongly Agree
I go through frequent periods of spiritual dryness.	0	15	20	7	29	25	4
My youth group is practically a part of my family.	0	0	15	8	24	27	26
I maintain regular personal devotions in addition to the things I prepare for youth programs.	1	5	11	3	28	27	26
I sometimes feel guilty taking a vacation to get away from my young people.	21	28	15	3	11	15	8
I often find I have nowhere to take my own problems.	12	26	14	3	16	20	9
I am often overwhelmed by the many responsibilities of youth work.	4	15	12	4	34	21	10

Figures have been rounded to the nearest whole percentage.

Summary

Over half the youth workers surveyed (65%) often feel overwhelmed with job stress. On top of that statistic, 45% feel alone with their problems. Among youth workers, the desire for intimacy seems almost as strong as it is among students.

In this chapter, Ridge examines the issues of sexual ethics, stress, guilt, and many other issues in which none of us are alone. As you consider your personal issues, ask yourself:

➤ What kinds of personal issues affect my ministry?

➤ Would my ethics pass a close spiritual audit?

➤ How am I dealing with stress and loneliness in my personal life?

Youth Workers Speak:

"The thing I like least about youth work is having problems that students cannot understand. I miss the fellowship of others my age. It's hard to grow as an adult when I continue to be a 'youth.'"

There are some things that affect me in youth ministry that no one knows about. They are not things that I can share in a prayer meeting, but things in my heart that are between me and God. However, I want to talk about some of these issues in this chapter.

We only hear about some of these issues—sexuality, finances, criticism—when a Christian leader makes an almost irreparable mistake. These personal issues can affect our moods and spirits so that we can no longer be effective in youth ministry. Perhaps it would be easier to discuss these topics outside the context of youth ministry, but unfortunately these issues are some of Satan's key weapons to destroy the Christian youth worker.

Sexual Ethics

As I watched the Jimmy Swaggart stories unfold on TV, my first reaction was one of anger. *Why*, I wondered, *would a servant like him with such a huge influence in worldwide Christianity, especially in Central America, be so insensitive that he would be willing to sacrifice his ministry for a few moments with a prostitute?*

As the stories began to develop and more details came out, I learned that Swaggart's problems went back as far as junior high school, when he began to feed an addiction to pornography that continued until it finally caught up with him in a hotel room with a prostitute. I began to understand a little bit more about Jimmy Swaggart and, frankly, felt a little empathy toward him.

I understand what it means to be tempted. If I were going to fall to temptation, it would probably be in the area of sensuality. God has wired me that way. There's something happening in the sexual behavior of youth workers that we must bring under control. Not long ago, I spoke at a youth pastor's conference where statistics were given that in that one denomination alone, 27 youth pastors had resigned their positions in the past year due to moral problems.

A few years ago a survey was done to find out why people leave ministry. One of the most interesting questions on the survey was: What is the greatest hindrance to your spirituality in the ministry? Women responded that their biggest problem is overcoming the desire to "mother" students into the kingdom of God. Men, on the other hand, said their number-one hindrance was their sexuality—their inability to control their emotions.

So how can I prevent sexual temptation from affecting my ministry?

There are some things I have to do to prevent myself from falling into the trap of sensuality. First, I take the Bible seriously when it commands me to flee sexual immorality (1 Corinthians 6:18). I believe that there are times and situations in which I simply can not minister. I may be tempted while on a retreat, in another city on a speaking assignment, or in a small group Bible study with students. Sometimes the situations have surprised me. I remember one such incident.

I was on a rather long, extensive speaking tour. At a conference in a northwest city, I found myself gravitating toward one particular woman in the crowd of 500. I had been traveling alone for a long time, so I decided to invite her to have lunch with me.

As we sat and ate, I began to realize that my motivation for spending time with her had nothing to do with ministry. It had to do with how I was feeling—I was lonely, tired, and I missed Robanne. At that point, I realized I was very vulnerable to becoming involved. And by the time our lunch was over, I realized the reason I was drawn to the woman was not because I was sexually attracted to her, but because she very much resembled my wife, Robanne.

When I became aware of the trap that I was placing myself

in, I became very concerned that I had become desensitized. I was surprised that I enjoyed talking with this woman. What did I learn from this situation? I learned I need to be very aware of how I feel and respond to someone of the opposite gender.

Second, I've learned to take charge of my sexual emotions. There are certain things I simply cannot talk to a woman about. I remember one particular counseling session in which one of my high school girls revealed that she was having sexual intercourse with several guys in her high school. I found myself asking more questions than I needed to in order to help this girl. I was not just intrigued by the story she was telling; I was fascinated by her exploits. That was terribly wrong. I was finally able to take charge of my emotions when I realized I was over the line.

My emotions get out of control when I don't have enough to do or when I am in a situation where I have too much time on my hands. Therefore, I take charge of my emotions by filling my time with things that are profitable, rather than letting relationships and activities wander in and out of my life.

Finally, I've learned to talk about these matters. I wonder what would have happened to Jimmy Swaggart had he had an opportunity to share confidentially with a group of men who could help him handle his struggle. I wonder if his loneliness forced him even deeper into the web of sin. I've found some people in my life whom I can talk to concerning this matter, and those people help keep me accountable to the objectives I have.

On Tuesday mornings I meet with a group of 10 men. We've been meeting for three years, and we've become more and more vulnerable with what we share. One morning, one of the men shared that he had asked his wife to cancel the movie channels from his cable TV. He found that he was becoming more and more tempted by watching sexually explicit films. His sharing allowed the rest of us to admit our struggles with similar matters. These men are able to ask me questions that other people are unable to ask, and I'm grateful for the accountability they bring to my life.

Financial Accountability

One of my senior pastors told me once that there are two things that get pastors in trouble—sex and money. We both decided that if we had to choose between the two, we'd pick sex. We also recognized that we are particularly vulnerable in the area of how we handle our funds.

For example, I often run two or three events at one time, such as a junior high retreat, a high school social, and maybe a college outing. On any given Sunday morning or Wednesday night, students hand me money. I end up having junior high money in the right front pocket, high school money in the left front pocket, and college money in the rear pocket.

After the Wednesday night meeting, I might take a few kids out for burgers. I get to the restaurant and have no personal money. So I rationalize taking some designated money out of one of my pockets, because after all I didn't turn in my mileage for the last year, and I have a few extra dollars due in reimbursements. So I just take it out here and call it even. Over the years, I've found myself doing more and more of that. Nothing big—$3 here, $5 there. Eating at McDonald's on church money. Still, that's wrong and somehow it always catches up with us.

Recently I heard from a former coworker. At one church he had used about $600 worth of church funds for personal use. The church found out about this and handled it in a wonderful way. They put him on probation for two years and made him pay back the money. Largely because of the way the church handled the situation, this young man has turned into a fine person.

But when I look back on my relationship with this man, I think the seeds of this unethical use of funds started in our early days of ministry together. In a few cases we said, "Oh, we can fudge here. We'll take a little money out of this account to pay for this account." Our actions didn't seem evil, just a little bit shady. Somehow we had developed some pretty intricate justifications for stealing.

So how do I maintain financial accountability in my ministry?

There are some things I do to prevent myself from falling into unethical handling of funds.

First of all, I have students make checks out to the church. Then everyone receives receipts with their canceled checks.

Second, I carry a receipt book at all times. If by some chance a student shows up with cash for an event, I make sure that money is recorded in duplicate so that there is no question about how much money has been received and where the money has gone.

Third, I've learned to delegate the handling of funds. My job places me in too many places at times. Therefore, I ask an adult sponsor or a reliable student to take care of the funds for special events. I rarely touch money now. That gives me less of an opportunity to justify the stealing that those of us in youth ministry sometimes fall into.

Finally, I try to keep accurate records. Occasionally, I request an internal audit from the church treasurer. Audits ensure that I do my best to account for every dime that comes in to the youth department.

Criticism

There is nothing that affects me more in life than criticism. For example, after I spoke at a very large youth conference, an evaluation was completed by all the participants. The directors of the conference sent me the results of these evaluations along with transcripts of the kids' comments.

The evaluations were unbelievably great. I was deeply affirmed by what some of the kids were saying. But there was one kid who apparently didn't like who I was, what I was saying, or how I said it. When I think about that event, that one kid is who I think about. I don't see the 500 great evaluations; I see the one that wasn't so flattering. That's how much criticism affects me.

So how do I cope with criticism in ministry?

Something happens in my heart (and in my ministry) when I receive criticism. I need to learn that criticism is always going to be part of ministry. In fact, without criticism, my ministry would probably be mediocre. People who don't cause waves get their steady raise and can stay at a church forever. But those of us in youth ministry who are pressing the limits of the church budget, facilities, and transportation system are going to be criticized.

What I've learned is that criticism may be appropriate for an effective ministry. I ought to be shaking up some kids and families, because as I present the claims of Jesus Christ, He is going to cause change. And change causes criticism.

I've learned two things to help me cope with criticism. First, I've learned that I respond to criticism by going off on tangents to please others. I do crazy things so I won't get criticized. As a result, I lose sight of where the Spirit of God is leading me.

Sometimes I meddle in areas of ministry where I have no business. I do this because it seems like a good way to keep the dogs at bay. One good example of this was when I organized the basketball leagues at a church in California. The junior high kids didn't feel like they had any athletic events, so I began a basketball program for them. Then the senior high guys came and said, "We'd like to do that, too." They were pretty vocal kids, so I decided it was easier to run the program than explain why I didn't want to spend another night out. Next, the senior girls came and said they wanted a league, too. So for three nights a week, I refereed basketball games. The only reason I went on this tangent was because I felt it was a way to keep criticism out of my life. Wrong motivation.

I need to look at my calendar and ask myself these questions: How many of these things am I doing because I feel God has called me to do them? How many of these things am I doing as a reaction to what people may think about me or my ministry?

A second thing I've learned about coping with criticism is that there is usually an element of truth in all criticism. Almost every youth worker is going to be accused of favoritism at one time or another. Perhaps there's an element of truth in that criticism. Maybe I *am* spending more time with a certain group of kids, and maybe the rest of the kids *do* feel neglected. This has certainly been true in my ministries. I hung out with three or four kids because they were fun to be around. They spent time with me, and they were committed to me. Sometimes our critics help us see the flaws in our ministry.

There are three questions that I ask myself when I am fighting critics:

> Is this an issue so big that I am willing to risk my entire career?
> Am I taking life too seriously?
> Am I trying to rally others in my defense to defeat my critic?

Stress

I'm a natural worrier. I worry about everything. I worry about kids arriving safely at meetings. I worry about parents. I worry about Robanne, my son R.W., and my daughter Barrett. I worry about my work and the fact that I've too many things to do and too little time to do them. All this worry creates a lot of stress for me.

For me, stress comes out in things like nail biting, tailgating, skipping meals, and grouchiness. These things occur not because I'm tired, but because I've got things on my mind. For example, one evening Robanne and I got a baby-sitter and went out to dinner for one of our family business meetings. By the middle of dinner, Robanne stopped me mid-sentence and asked, "Ridge, you don't want to be here, do you?"

That wasn't really true. I wanted to spend time with Robanne, but I knew I had three deadlines the next day that were more important to me than trying to decide whether or not we should visit Robanne's parents the next week.

Work is another source of stress for me. For example, I don't like facing the finance committee to talk about budget cuts when the church is not making its budget. I remember at one of my former churches where I got so stressed out after a staff meeting that I actually threw up on the way back to my office.

So how do I manage stress and its effect on my life and ministry?

I don't handle stress very well. When I'm stressed out, I get angry, I meddle, and I procrastinate. When my life is characterized by those three things, I know that what I need to do is work at solving the *real* problems. One of the ways I manage stress in my life is by being spiritually prepared for battle.

I have tried to develop some discipline in terms of worship and praise in my devotional life. I find that when I am spending time with God, learning and growing in my own personal walk, my stress level seems to be reduced. Somehow, God rearranges my life and gives me strength. When I feel as if God is in control, I feel less stress.

But when things seem like they're on top of me, and I can't seem to get them under my control, I get stressed out. Those are the times I find myself less able to handle things that come up during the day. An hour of worship, praise, and prayer with God in the morning helps me put the issues that I need to handle in perspective.

I also need to pick my battles carefully. When I'm stressed out, I feel like arguing about everything with everyone. But wise youth workers put themselves on the line for only those issues that help them accomplish their goals.

Another area that causes me stress is poor work habits. I have spent a lot of hours doing nothing in the name of ministry. I've spent a lot of time on tasks where I get so distracted that I ignore more important objectives. So, I've worked on developing a better time management program.

Finally, when it comes to stress, I take the model of Christ seriously. When Christ was wrongly accused before Pilate, His response was silence. When I'm involved in a stressful situation, particularly church or parents' meetings that could potentially backfire, I need to say as few words as possible. This action will keep me from creating conflicts for myself.

I also try to reduce stress by listening to my body. Am I eating properly? Am I exercising? Am I getting enough sleep? My body may be saying, "You need to stop and look after me for a while!"

Guilt

If I had a stronger sense of guilt about the sin in my life, I would probably be motivated to live a purer life. Unfortunately, most of the guilt I feel is unhealthy or related to the way others perceive me.

The other day I was playing golf with a friend who had arrived from the East Coast to visit the Center for Student Missions. While we were playing golf, I kept thinking, *I hope nobody sees me. It's Thursday afternoon, and they might think I have no business being on the golf course.*

The only person I met was another pastor who was playing

hooky as well. That made me feel a little better. But I shouldn't have to feel guilty at all. Most of my work time is on weekends, and I deserve to be able to play golf every once in a while, even if it's on a Thursday afternoon.

When Robanne and I are walking around a mall, sometimes I feel guilty if I have a shopping bag from an expensive store. *What if we meet people from the church? They may think we are making too much money since we can afford to shop at such an expensive store.*

I feel guilty for owning a home when someone moves into our community and can't afford one because the cost of housing in Southern California is so high. I feel guilty even though I bought my home when prices were reasonable.

So how do I deal with guilt?

There's a lot of false guilt attached to youth ministry because we *think* people have certain expectations for us. But most of these expectations are self-imposed. To fight these feelings, I've set some boundaries on how hard I work. First of all, I'm required to work only 40 hours a week. However, most youth ministry programs take more time than that. I need to keep track of my hours so I'm not letting the ministry get the best of me while Robanne gets the leftovers.

I also try to write clear-cut goals and objectives that let me evaluate my work. I don't judge my job performance by what I'm feeling at any particular time. I review myself on an annual basis and determine whether or not the goals and objectives I set have been met. If I can reach those goals and objectives (and still play golf once a week on a Thursday afternoon), then I don't feel guilty anymore. Of course, those goals and objectives need to be communicated to the congregation so that when they do see me playing golf, they know that I'm still on track.

I also need to recognize that my job will never be finished, no matter how guilty I feel. There's always one more kid to talk to, one more flier to produce, one more phone call to make, one more event to plan, one more seminar to attend. A youth minister doesn't have to work to the point of exhaustion in order to live with his or her conscience.

Failure

I've had some failure in my years of youth ministry. I've done some things that have just not worked, and I've made some serious financial errors. For example, I've never been real great at running high school social events. In fact, to be quite honest, I'm pretty bad at running socials. I do much better with planning mission trips and retreats. Parties are not my idea of a good time, so I've usually delegated the planning of these events to somebody who likes to do them.

However, I remember planning a student banquet for a celebration at the end of the school year. I spent a lot of money on decorations and getting it together. I got all the parents involved, and nobody came. I felt like a failure.

Another time, our local network of youth pastors put together a big outreach program. We brought in a well-known speaker and a band. We worked hard on publicity and were expecting thousands of kids. On the three nights we ran this big event, we must have had less than 150 students in attendance. There were almost more of us youth pastors and sponsors than there were students. The event was a failure.

Everybody in the youth pastors' group knew it, but nobody would say it. I justified it by saying, "It was just the wrong place at the wrong time," and "I guess this event will just set us up for doing some good things next year when kids can catch the vision." I was afraid to admit that the event was a failure.

So how do I handle failures in my ministry?

I feel tremendous pressure to be successful. At times, my ministry may become a showcase instead of place were I can minister to others. This pressure to succeed is fed by competition and the idea that bigger is better. I need to remember that some kids may not come to my youth group for reasons that have nothing to do with me. For instance, they may not attend because their friends go to a different church.

I also feel tremendous pressure to succeed for the sake of job security. Youth programs that aren't doing well cause rumbles in the church, and rumbles in the church create major stress for the leadership, and that stressed-out leadership causes trouble for me.

The reality is that at least three or four times a year, I'm going to do something that's not going to work. I need to stop denying that failure is part of youth ministry. The biggest problem with the whole notion that failure *isn't* part of youth ministry can be summed up in one word—*pride*. Youth workers, generally speaking, are pretty proud people.

We need to start approaching our ministry from a position of weakness rather than strength. Occasionally, I write a column for *Youthworker Journal*. Whenever I talk about feeling insecure, weak, and jealous—failures that are part of my youth ministry—I am amazed at the number of people who tell me how much those columns speak to them. Other times I write about great ideas for youth ministry, but I hardly ever receive responses on those columns.

Loneliness

Youth ministry often produces feelings of loneliness. I've had the benefit of working with some wonderful senior pastors, but

I have not been able to avoid the loneliness of what it feels like to be a couple without friends.

I remember the day that Robanne and I realized that other couples were buying nice homes and moving up the corporate ladder, while we were still running lock-ins at the church. We waited 11½ years before we had our first child. We felt pretty lonely because most of our friends were having children. Sometimes we felt that life was passing us by while everyone else was experiencing the world. I was disappointed once when our friends all packed up and went to a condo in Florida and, of course, we didn't have the money or the time to go with them.

So how do I deal with loneliness in ministry?

The first step in dealing with loneliness is to recognize that we are lonely people. We all have the basic need to belong, to have community.

Loneliness was part of Jesus' ministry. Jesus and His disciples felt lonely, and yet they took some steps to remedy these feelings. They traveled together, built relationships, and became a team. This is what Robanne and I attempted to do. We knew we couldn't fit into the Homebuilders' Class at church because the high school class was meeting at the same time. So we built a support group with our high school staff. Every Tuesday night, we opened our home for a potluck dinner where we shared and prayed together. Those people became our good friends. They bore our burdens, and when our son R.W. was born, they made a friendship quilt for our wall.

We beat the loneliness factor because we had built a staff of people who cared about each other and functioned as a team. Our relationships created a very attractive environment that helped us in our effort to reach kids.

Small Church Spotlight

Codependency is the biggest personal issue that affects my ministry. I'm the kind of person who develops addictive-type relationships with people or things, resulting in dysfunctional behavior. As I've become more aware of the hurts in my past, I've also painfully begun to grasp how my codependence has sabotaged my ministry with students. For example, at times my self-esteem has been so fragile that when a student rejected me, I felt a hidden desire to punish that student for hurting me. And in a small youth group, that kind of behavior does not go unnoticed.

But perhaps the greatest saboteur is my not being able to set functional boundaries or fences to prevent students from invading my space or to keep me from invading their territories. I have trouble saying no and setting limits for students because I fear their rejection. On the other hand, I sometimes step into students' lives, trying to control or manipulate them, especially under the guise of spiritual concern. These behaviors usually result in anger, resentment, and/or shame.

As I continue in my recovery from codependency, I have begun moving away from these lifelong behaviors. Obviously I'm not perfect, and I feel guilty about the way I've treated students at times. But as I share my journey to becoming a healthier person with my students, I have the hope of receiving their forgiveness and of halting any perpetuation of their dysfunctions.

Scripture Meditation

"Are they servants of Christ? (I am out of my mind to talk like this.) I am more. I have worked much harder, been in prison more frequently, been flogged more severely, and been exposed to death again and again. Five times I received from the Jews the forty lashes minus one. Three times I was beaten with rods, once I was stoned, three times I was shipwrecked, I spent a night and a day in the open sea, I have been constantly on the move. I have been in danger from rivers, in danger from bandits, in danger from my own countrymen, in danger from Gentiles; in danger in the city, in danger in the country, in danger at sea; and in danger from false brothers. I have labored and toiled and have often gone without sleep; I have known hunger and thirst and have often gone without food; I have been cold and naked. Besides everything else, I face daily the pressure of my concern for all the churches. Who is weak, and I do not feel weak? Who is led into sin, and I do not inwardly burn?

"If I must boast, I will boast of the things that show my weakness" (2 Corinthians 11:23-30).

Spend some time meditating on what God has to say to you. Use the following questions to study this passage.

1. Why did Paul resort to boasting in this passage?

2. Can you relate to any of Paul's experiences?

3. How do the things that you have suffered or experienced validate or affect your ministry to students?

4. Have you identified your personal weaknesses? If so, have you "boasted" of those weaknesses as a witness of God's grace and strength in your life?

Father, help me to realize that "when I am weak, then I am strong."

PROGRAMS

You and Your Programs

	Strongly Disagree	Disagree	Somewhat Disagree	Undecided	Agree	Somewhat Agree	Strongly Agree
I try to keep all or most of my programs running throughout the summer.	1	5	4	5	21	33	29
I have trouble finding good resources on many of the topics I'd like to teach.	13	33	20	12	15	6	11
It's harder to find good materials for Bible study than for social activities and "fun stuff."	5	21	16	11	13	28	5

Figures have been rounded to the nearest whole percentage.

Summary

When asked about programs and resources, most youth workers surveyed said they had little or no problem finding resource materials for their programs. However, 42% admitted they had some difficulty finding good Bible study material.

In this chapter, Ridge talks about the importance of meeting the needs of students through programs and resources. As you consider your programs, ask yourself:

➤ How do I know I'm meeting the various needs of individual students?

➤ How do I measure the success of my programs?

➤ Where does Sunday School fit in my youth program?

Youth Workers Speak:

"When I started in youth ministry, my philosphy was: Fun will bring kids out. Now I believe Christ will bring kids out. I've become less concerned about the size of my group and more deeply concerned about discipleship and Bible study for each youth."

The problem with following a program is that it becomes routine. There are things we must do every week, month, or year, such as Sunday School, Bible studies, retreats, summer camp. When the activities become routine, we lose our creativity.

Those of us in youth ministry sometimes have the misperception that all programs have to be exciting, fun, something we really want to do. But in reality there are some unglamorous activities we are required to lead, and it's not uncommon for us to perceive these programs as stale and boring.

I felt that way about our Sunday School program. Kids came and seemed to enjoy it, but I was bored. I was tired of having to prepare for an activity that I wasn't pumped up about, but I couldn't ignore the fact that God continued to bless it. In this chapter, I want to talk about the kinds of programs that excite a youth worker and those that may create some stress.

Programs That Meet Needs

A few of the youth programs I've run have not worked. Sometimes it's because kids aren't interested in participating. Sometimes it's because I'm not prepared or the curriculum has not come. However, most programs that are directed toward students' needs will be successful, regardless of their format.

Kids will attend programs that have three elements: risk, adventure, and significance. Kids need to feel that what they are doing puts them on the edge. *Can I really succeed at this?* kids ask. *Is this a cool activity?* That's why some of the wildest, zaniest games we play seem to work so well. Kids like the risk of balancing eggs on their heads or swallowing something that looks gross.

Kids also want adventure. Like their youth workers, they want to break out of the routine. They like canoe trips, rock climbing, wild camps, and amusement parks. The more opportunity for adventure, the better the kids like it.

Kids also want to feel some significance in what they do. I try to provide programs where kids are participants rather than spectators. Missions programs have worked well for me. The training sessions leading up to these mission trips have provided me with some great ministry opportunities with kids.

Other programs like the ones provided by the Center for Student Missions allow kids to feed a hungry person, experience what it means to be homeless, and live in a hotel that would be undesirable for most people to live in. It's these kinds of experiences that help kids to feel a sense of significance.

The program that has been the most significant in my youth ministry has been Sidewalk Sunday School, an after-school day-care program for latchkey kids housed at a local apartment complex. My high school students raised money, wrote the curriculum, directed the activities, and built relationships with the people in the apartment complex as well as with the latchkey kids and their families. There's great joy in producing programs that meet the needs of kids.

So how can I have better programming in my ministry?

I have experienced no better feeling in youth ministry than to run a program or meeting that really meets needs in kids' lives. It seems to me that effective youth programs have four common elements. First, the program must fill a need in the student's life. For example, I have a small group that I'm working with right now. Each week I look forward to getting together with these high school guys. We study the Bible inductively, and it seems to be working well. Those guys really need the support of each other, and the small group meets that need.

One of the ways I know a program is going well is when kids have a sense of ownership. They begin to choose church programs over school activities and are filled with anticipation for the youth events. A healthy group self-image develops.

Second, every youth program, whether it's a small group or a retreat, needs an adequately trained staff running it. I need to help my staff be prepared and know exactly what's going on.

For example, on youth retreats I used to spend so much time making sure that we had transportation, lodging, food, speaker, recreation, music, and so on that I just assumed the staff would know what they were supposed to do. Now, about two or three weeks before the retreat, I get the staff together for a Saturday morning where I walk them through the retreat. What I've found is that most of the staff appreciate knowing what is going to happen and how they can get involved and be more effective in ministry to the kids. In addition, I give the staff opportunity in the preparation process to be creative, and they usually have ideas that can enhance the retreat.

Third, an effective youth program produces results in kids. It's up to the individual youth worker to define what his expectations are for those results. I could expect a particular program to result in stronger personal commitments or just open sharing where kids are able to air their feelings.

Finally, I always try to make sure that the students and I leave meetings and youth programs feeling like we had a good time being with one another. I don't mean that the programs aren't serious. I just mean that the meetings should produce a comfortable atmosphere where we can learn and have fun together.

Programs That Fail

I get really frustrated when I plan a program and nobody comes. At two of my churches, I tried a couple of times to get a high school choir started. But neither of the youth groups that I worked with in those churches were interested in forming a choir. Unfortunately, all of my efforts met with failure because nobody came. That made me feel pretty discouraged.

I've also had problems generating interest in confirmation or pastor's classes for kids. It's so disappointing to work really hard writing creative curriculum and have a low attendance.

For some reason, kids in my youth groups have never strongly attended the socials I've planned. I am always discouraged when I spend time and money trying to produce something that apparently there was no need to do.

So how do I deal with programs that fail?

I usually ask the following questions when a program fails due to lack of student involvement:

Why didn't students attend this event?

What caused this event to fail?

Was it something I did?

Was it ill timed?

Was it not a good idea in the first place?

Could I have recruited someone else to do this same program and increased its potential for success?

Should I try this event again? If so, how can I change or rearrange it to make it successful?

Here are four things I do to find out why kids are not attending programs or events:

First, I ask the kids who aren't coming to programs why they aren't involved. For example, in a phone survey, I ask them to describe the first thing that comes to mind when they hear the words *Sunday School, youth group, church, worship service,* and so on.

Second, I ask the active kids why their friends don't come to programs. For example, I ask the kids to complete this sentence: "My friends would come to this youth group if the group would ... "

Third, I ask the parents of the inactive kids why their kids don't come. For instance, I really wanted Joy to be part of my youth group. So I asked her dad what I needed to do to get Joy to come to the Wednesday night meeting. He said, "Pick her up once." I hadn't realized that Joy didn't know anyone in the youth group and just needed an entry point. So I picked her up and spent some time with her, and sure enough, she became a part of the group.

Last but not least, I ask myself the following questions:

What is it about my youth group that makes it unappealing to some kids?

What causes kids to leave?

Why isn't this program successful?

In my first youth ministry, I ran a program called Walk This Way. It was a three-day conference for students that took place in our church gym. Twelve hundred students attended the first year. The next year we lined up a good speaker and great music. We were excited about what God was going to do at this conference, but to our surprise, only 150 people showed up the first night. I felt embarrassed, like a failure, even a little bit mad at God.

I've learned that part of youth ministry is running programs that don't work. For some reason, we in ministry feel that everything we do must be successful or God is not in it.

Sunday School

Almost every church has a Sunday School, and with that Christian Education program comes the assumption that youth will be involved in it. Being responsible for 52 lessons a year in a meeting where many kids are forced to come is probably one of the most difficult tasks for any youth pastor.

So how do I deal with Sunday School in youth ministry?

At my second church, I decided to make Sunday School my

outreach time. I did a survey of students in the community and found that Sunday morning was the time when students had the fewest commitments during the week. My only competitors were things like "Face the Nation" and fishing shows on ESPN. I spent time being as creative as I possibly could. I recognized that Sunday School needed to be a very important part of my planning, so I developed a good staff and a format that was fun for kids.

We turned a program that had the potential to be a boring meeting where kids were required to come into a major outreach time where I saw kids come to know the Lord. I think youth pastors need to change their attitudes about this traditional program. They may discover that this prime time on Sunday mornings can be turned into profitable time.

One of the difficulties I've had with Sunday School is getting kids to talk and discuss issues in that setting. Mike Yaconelli and Scott Koenigsaecker in their book *Get 'Em Talking* (Zondervan, 1989) have five ground rules for a great discussion.

1. What is said stays in this room.

2. No put-downs, and that includes sarcasm and unkind remarks.

3. There is no such thing as a dumb question.

4. No one is forced to talk.

5. Only one person talks at a time.

These kinds of rules have facilitated a better discussion between students and myself.

Small Church Spotlight

The youth programs at a small church are not usually very elaborate. In large churches, many youth events or programs can be run simultaneously and still be effective. But in a small church, I've learned to be more selective about programming.

One year, I ran a Bible study on Monday night and a youth group meeting on Wednesday night and expected students to be at Sunday School for another Bible study. Attendance dropped at all three activities because students were overdosing on Bible study and each other. I was frustrated and overwhelmed by having to prepare studies for three programs only to have three or four students show up. By scaling back to one meeting outside of Sunday School and changing the focus of each program, students' attendance increased and my frustration decreased.

Now I select programs based on the following process:

1. Determine which students I want to minister to and what

their spiritual needs are. This can be done through informal discussion, surveys, and research.

2. Determine which needs our small church can meet.

3. Set goals to meet those students' specific needs.

4. List available resources including people, facilities, finances, curriculum, etc.

5. Identify and implement the best programs possible given the available resources to meet students' specific needs.

6. Evaluate the effectiveness of programs using students' and other involved adults' input.

Scripture Meditation

"Not many of you should presume to be teachers, my brothers, because you know that we who teach will be judged more strictly" (James 3:1).

Spend some time meditating on what God has to say to you. Use the following questions to study this passage.

1. Why do you think James cautioned us on presuming to be teachers?

2. Why will teachers be "judged more strictly"?

3. How seriously do you take your teaching responsibilities?

4. Are there parts of your teaching program that need improvement?

Father, help me to remember that I am accountable to You when I'm leading Your people.

YOUTH GROUPS

You and Your Youth Group

	Strongly Disagree	Disagree	Somewhat Disagree	Undecided	Agree	Somewhat Agree	Strongly Agree
My youth group members have a strong commitment to each other.	0	4	12	9	39	28	8
For the most part, I am pleased with the spiritual maturity of my group.	3	11	25	5	33	21	1
I think I could be more effective if I had a smaller group to work with.	15	30	16	16	12	9	1
My group expects too much of me.	8	34	18	24	8	7	1

Figures have been rounded to the nearest whole percentage.

Summary

When asked about their students' spiritual commitment, 55% of the youth workers surveyed were satisfied with the spiritual growth in their youth group. Only 22% felt that they could be more effective if their youth group were smaller. Of those surveyed, the average size of high school groups was 41 students; the average size of junior high groups was 31 students; and the average size of a combined high school/junior high school group was 86 students. However, sizes of youth groups ranged from 6 students to 550 students.

In this chapter, Ridge examines some of the most common problems with youth groups—conflicts and cliques. As you read about these and other youth group issues, ask yourself:

➤ How can I help my youth group have more meaningful spiritual experiences?

➤ How do I deal with conflicts and cliques in my youth group?

➤ Am I caught up in the myth that "bigger is better" when it comes to *my* youth group?

Youth Workers Speak:

"The things I like least about youth work are cliques, half-committed kids, and apathy."

Youth ministry is not a one-on-one discipleship relationship. Our primary work is with youth *groups*. Often kids need to get comfortable with their role in the youth group before they become theologically involved. That is to say, before I talk to students about God, they have to be at ease with the people in the room.

For example, if I take junior high kids on a retreat and don't tell them who is in their cabin, I can expect great dissonance until they discover their roommates for the weekend. The need to fit in is what makes it so difficult to deal with kids from broken homes. They lack the ability to build good relationships and to work as part of a team. I've found that the way to improve on those skills and abilities is to provide some group experiences.

Mountaintop Experiences

I live for mountaintop experiences where everything goes right in the youth group. For example, I really enjoy a retreat where the speaker is effective, the band is good, the kids get along, and the staff works well. Usually the kids end up with an extremely powerful spiritual experience. I also get high on missions trips where kids share what God has done in their lives and what they want to do when they go back home.

I know there are problems with those kinds of experiences, but I have to admit too that those experiences of seeing kids broken and sensitive to the Spirit of God are what keep me going in youth ministry. Kids come away from mountaintop experiences with their arms around one another, ready to serve and be committed to Christ. The unity that is experienced there is so infrequent in their groups that I feel mountaintop experiences are basic to helping students understand what true unity is all about.

On my very first mission trip to Mexico, I remember how uptight I was about taking kids across the border. After a great week of ministry, we ended with a chapel program and communion service. During the service, I was doing some preparation for the next week, when one of my student leaders found me and said, "Ridge, you need to come and be part of this. This is really neat!"

So I went over to where the kids were having their communion service, and I could not believe what I saw. Not only were there tears, commitments, and open sharing, but there was a meeting of God like I have never seen before. To this day, 17 years later, I still get emotional, still feel a sense of bonding with those kids because of what God did in that circle of communion. I will never forget that moment. It has become a watershed by which I evaluate all other experiences.

Of course, when the kids returned to the States, some of them fell away, some grew, and some just remained the same. The experience had various meanings for them, but for me, it was a great mountaintop experience.

So how can I create more mountaintop experiences for my youth group?

I've found there are some things that make these kinds of experiences *really* happen. First, I must help bring kids' emotions to the surface by putting them into situations that stir up their lives—situations outside their environment, culture, social status, etc. I've watched big, rugged football players show incredible tenderness when God is working in their lives.

Second, I need to challenge my youth group to a higher commitment. They make promises to God, to me, to their parents, and to themselves, and I know that they won't keep all those promises. But it's wonderful to see those kids stand up. Whether or not those commitments will last, it just feels so right when kids make promises to God and each other. It brings unity to the group.

Third, I need to help my students be broken for God. Often

they feel broken because they have been disobedient and they want to make a change in their lives. They truly want to repent, but they aren't often in situations where their disobedience or insensitivity are challenged.

The biggest problem with mountaintop experiences is the deflation that comes afterward. I struggle because I want kids to continue living with the same sense of joy and commitment that they experienced at camp or on that mission trip.

Valley Experiences

A few years ago I made arrangements for my youth group and their parents to help an inner-city mission by doing a fundraising banquet. Our job was to bring all the food and set up decorations and tables. The director of the mission was to secure the band and the speaker.

I felt this was one way that a suburban white church could link with the black inner-city ministry to help get things done. The day came for us to deliver the food to the banquet hall we had rented. We were to arrive at 5:30 P.M., and the banquet was to begin at 7:30 P.M. By 7:00 P.M. everything was in order. All the places were set. We expected over 300 people. The problem was that no one showed up. The mission director had not done his homework in inviting enough people, even though we had printed up invitations. The youth group pointed to me, asking, "How come no one came? What are we going to do with all this chicken?"

Another valley experience occurred during a missions training session. The student leaders had not done their homework and were totally unprepared when we met together. I remember blowing up and telling them that if they couldn't do the job they had agreed to do, I would just have to cancel the trip.

So how do I deal with valley experiences?

After valley experiences I try to do the three A's of youth ministry. First, I *admit* to God and myself that I have made a mistake and that my attitude is wrong. Then I *apologize* to the students and ask for their forgiveness. Finally I *ask for help* and remove the source of the problem.

When I arrived at my third church, there was already a large youth group. Their popular youth pastor had left suddenly, and my job was to restore morale and rebuild a successful youth ministry. There were lots of kids coming, but the youth ministry was organized in a way that I wasn't comfortable with. The best-attended program of the youth ministry was on Wednesday night, and it included 10-year-olds through 35-year-olds.

The Wednesday night service was built on worship, and quite frankly, it was a neat experience. But to be effective, we needed to get the junior high kids in their own program, high school kids in their own meetings, and college students and young marrieds in their own groups. To rebuild the youth ministry meant changing how we ministered to people. As a result, a lot of people left the youth programs. On a short-term basis, it was very difficult for me and the church. But strategically, I think the church and youth programs were greatly improved and became more effective at reaching individuals.

Conflict in the Youth Group

It was only the second retreat that I had ever done in my whole life. I had gone to a camp in northern California with about 35 students from our church. The camp was so remote that we had to take a snowcat to get there because the roads were closed. In fact, it was so isolated the kids felt a little trapped in the camp, and this isolation somehow accelerated some of the conflicts in the youth group.

The speaker was very good on Friday night, and the Saturday meetings were really exciting. God seemed to be working. But on Sunday morning, only half the kids appeared at the communion service, which was supposed to be a great time of unity. After some investigation, I discovered that a major grudge between Jill and Tracey, two girls in the youth group, had apparently escalated during the weekend, resulting in the no-shows.

I've come to recognize that my ministry is influenced by the conflict in my youth group. Sometimes the disunity, disrespect, and lack of response to my teaching has nothing to do with my efforts. It has to do with the conflicts in the youth group. In this case, when I saw the problem with Jill and Tracey, I was able to solve the problem of unity in our group.

Conflicts in youth groups can absolutely devastate an event. They can also create a relational dissonance that affects a student's ability to communicate with God. Sometimes conflicts revolve around romance. Someone has designs on another kid and things don't work out. Or self-esteem. I remember one youth trip where a big conflict broke out because the girls were taking too much time in the only available bathroom in order to look good for doing ministry. The guys were really frustrated. The issue wasn't the time being spent in the showers, but whether the girls were right to place so much importance on their appearance. Some guys thought they were just being vain. Gossip is another conflict starter. Someone spreads stories about another kid, and pretty soon factions build and begin to tear the youth group down.

So how do I deal with conflict in the youth group?

In my ministry I've always used three ways to deal with conflicts between youth group members. My first rule is to deal only with the people directly involved in the situation rather than the whole group. My second rule is to identify what the problem really is. Gossip or lack of respect for others may disguise a problem of self-esteem, bitterness, or anger. My third rule is to agree together with everyone involved in the situation on a solution. We come up with a game plan to solve the problem.

In the situation with Jill and Tracey, I isolated the two girls and told them that I knew they were the center of the problem and that I would talk to them a little bit later. Before the communion service started, I talked about unity with the kids who were not involved in the problem.

Youth Group Cliques

For every 10 people in my youth group, a subgroup seems to form. If I have 30 kids in my youth group, I usually have three separate sociological groups I need to minister to. When those groups become exclusive, I have a problem called *cliques*.

One of my larger youth groups was filled with cliques. Because North High School had an outstanding athletic program, the kids from Central High School felt as if they were second-class citizens and kept to themselves. The Christian school kids were yet another clique.

The youth group at my current church is made up of surfers. If you don't like the beach, if you're not into the water, you probably won't fit into our youth group. I've seen problems between soccer players and non-soccer players, between students from different schools, between students who are into computers and those who are computer illiterate.

So how do I deal with cliques in the youth group?

One of the ways that I solved the problem of cliques was to change my attitude toward them. Instead of trying to break down cliques, I put them into small groups with staff people who were part of each clique's world. For example, a Christian school teacher might be assigned to work with Christian school kids. Then I worked with the staff to help them communicate to the kids that they could build unity in the body of Christ.

But the best way that I know to break down cliques within youth groups is to travel together. Long trips to winter retreats, summer camp, and missions trips break down walls better than anything I know. I think that's why Jesus traveled with His disciples—it broke down a lot of the barriers between fishermen and tax collectors.

Small Church Spotlight

In a small church with only four or five kids in my youth group, how do I get beyond a feeling of inadequacy? Here are four myths about the size of youth groups.

1. Bigger is better. Success is equated with big cars, big houses, and big paychecks. But in the kingdom of God, quantity has nothing to do with quality. Jesus chose the images of the little and the lost to represent the family of God. He's not impressed with bigness.

2. Nothing works with a small youth group. That's not true. Most of Ridge's ministry has been spent trying to turn large youth groups into smaller, more manageable youth groups. What can he do with 100 kids? Put them into small groups of four or five with one adult who cares about them. While there are real drawbacks to small groups, there are also tremendous benefits.

3. If my youth group is small, there must be something wrong.

If my youth group is big, that doesn't mean God is blessing it. If a church has 1,000 members, the youth pastor ought to have 100 kids in the youth group. But if my church has 75 people and I have a dozen high school kids, my group may be attracting a higher percentage of the youth than the larger church group.

4. The primary objective of a small youth group is growth in numbers. How wrong to think that as long as I'm adding new people to the group, I'm being effective. Any youth group should have a primary goal of bringing its membership—large or small—to a better relationship with Jesus Christ.

I've worked with a youth group of 50 students and a youth group of 10 students. There are many activities that are conducive to either size group. There are also both benefits and disadvantages to working with small and large youth groups.

Scripture Meditation

"As Jesus was walking beside the Sea of Galilee, he saw two brothers, Simon called Peter and his brother Andrew. They were casting a net into the lake, for they were fishermen. 'Come, follow me,' Jesus said, 'and I will make you fishers of men.' At once they left their nets and followed him. . . .

"Now when he saw the crowds, he went up on a mountainside and sat down. His disciples came to him, and he began to teach them" (Matthew 4:18-20; 5:1-2).

Spend some time meditating on what God has to say to you. Use the following questions to study this passage.

1. Why do you think Jesus called the disciples to follow Him?

2. What was unusual about the disciples' responses?

3. Do you consider the students in your youth group your disciples?

4. What are you doing to help your students become "fishers of men"?

5. How can you apply the principles of discipleship found in these verses with your youth group?

Father, make me a fisher of students as I teach them to be fishers for You.

CHAPTER 8

FAMILY

You and Your Family

	Strongly Disagree	Disagree	Somewhat Disagree	Undecided	Somewhat Agree	Agree	Strongly Agree
I include my spouse/family in youth activities whenever possible.	0	8	6	9	12	32	33
Several times my involvement with youth work has been a major source of conflict in my marriage.	12	26	12	16	24	5	5
Youth work takes away time I should be spending with my spouse/children.	5	14	14	19	31	9	9
It's difficult to have a normal home life when involved in youth work.	8	21	18	5	24	12	12

Figures have been rounded to the nearest whole percentage.

Summary

Though many youth workers (48%) find it difficult to have a normal home life, only 34% admit that their involvement in youth work is a source of marital conflict. Perhaps we should have surveyed their spouses to get a different perspective.

In this chapter, Ridge shares some personal experiences with family issues. As you read about these, ask yourself:

➤ Am I spending adequate time with my spouse and family?

➤ How do I maintain schedules in my ministry and home life?

➤ How can I prevent youth ministry from completely taking over my personal life?

Youth Workers Speak:

"I'm tired of not having enough time or hours in a day. Night activities conflict with evening family times. I don't like having my children be disrespectful to me during youth meetings."

I have really had two youth ministry careers—before children and after children. In some very practical ways, the youth group was Robanne's and my family before we had our own children. But now with a son and daughter, we feel a little bit more selfish about our family time, space, and resources. It didn't use to bother us when youth would wake us up at night. But now the evening is very precious time to Robanne and our family. Having a wife and children has definitely made a difference in my ministry.

Days Off with the Family

I tend to be a workaholic. It is nothing for me to work 75–80 hours a week. Part of the problem is that I never feel my job is complete, so I'm always adding more and more activities to my life. And the people who get the short end are my family. I have a hard time saying no. If somebody calls me up and wants me to write or speak or come over and visit their kid, I'll drop what I'm doing to please that person.

What I'm really saying is that sometimes I'm not as good at time management as I should be. I usually have several uncompleted tasks going at the same time. Those uncompleted tasks cause me to waste a lot of time. I find myself working in 15-20 minute intervals. A phone call will interrupt me, someone will come in my office, or I begin a conversation at the coffee pot. All these interruptions send me in various directions. If I could get eight hours' worth of work done in eight hours I would be a far better youth worker.

So how do I learn to preserve my days off from ministry?

I've learned that when I *do* work at the church I need to divide my time into two-hour increments. During those two hours, I do specifically what is required to accomplish or complete a given task. This prevents me from wasting time and having to work on my day off.

I've also developed four rules for preserving my day off.

Rule #1—I leave my work at the office on my day off. I don't bring home my briefcase. I don't get up early and look at what I could be doing. I don't call or stop by my office during my day off. If I stop by just to check the mail, I'll be there an hour. I don't take phone calls unless they are emergencies. On my day off I totally drop out of ministry to the church and minister only to my family.

Rule #2—I plan my day off with my family one week in advance. If I know a week ahead of time that we're going to Disneyland, I have less tendency to fit tasks into my schedule on my day off. If I don't have any plans, I will fill that time vacuum with urgent needs of the church.

I also have to schedule one day every so often to work around the house. I do that in addition to the day off that I take with my family. The house needs to be painted, the lawn needs to be mowed, and the cars need to be serviced. I try to make sure those maintenance jobs don't infringe on my family time.

Rule #3—I try not to skip my devotions on my day off. Devotions help me think more about my family. I pray for them before they get up, and that allows me to approach my day off in a more spiritual way.

Rule #4—I am as creative on my day off as I am in youth ministry. When I think about how carefully I plan a retreat to make sure that kids are entertained, ministered to, and challenged in their faith, I am embarrassed at how little time and creative energy I spend helping my family enjoy those same kinds of experiences. Therefore, I try to be creative with my family time.

Family Time Conflicts

Since most of my meetings with laypeople take place in the

evening, I have to learn how to best organize my time, attend those meetings, and not abandon my family.

Now that we have children, Robanne is not traveling with me as often as in the past. Robanne would like to get away and spend some time in ministry with students, but because I travel so much, the last thing I want to do is go on a trip. I'd rather work around the house. We're just now beginning to learn how to accommodate each other's needs.

We have never allowed students to stay in our home on a regular basis. We don't have Bible studies or meetings in our home except on very rare occasions. We've even communicated to kids that we do not want them to call us on Saturday evenings. That's the time when I get ready for Sunday morning. Our home is open to kids who have emergencies, and they're welcome to come at any time. Still, we would rather the kids think about the church building when they have a need. I know this is different from the views of other youth pastors, but separating our home from our work has helped keep our family life strong.

So how do I deal with those things that conflict with my family time?

Whenever I have evening meetings, I feel permission to take off the mornings and spend that time with my family. That kind of arrangement gives me the opportunity to impact my family's lives as well as maintain the kinds of meetings that are required to run a youth ministry. I also recognize that the lay people with whom I am working are sacrificing time with their families as well. That motivates me to have shorter, succinct meetings.

Occasionally I have a committee meeting on a night where entire families are present for club meetings or choir practice. By combining these events into one evening, it frees up more time during the week for everybody else.

157

Spouses

When I think about some of the gifts God has given me, the greatest gift has been my wife, Robanne. I don't say this because it's what youth pastors are supposed to say. I say this because she has adapted perfectly to my lifestyle and workstyle. I think we complement each other very well. She enjoys kids and being around them, but she's not highly involved in youth ministry. She doesn't mind sharing me with the kids and with the leadership of the church.

Right now there is a youth pastor in my area who is very talented. But his wife has a hard time with authority and anyone who is supervising her family. While the youth pastor's job performance is sterling, the church may have to let him go or ask him to make some adjustments in his ministry because of the wife's problems.

So how do I effectively involve my spouse in ministry?

I have no rules for involving Robanne in my ministry except that she only has to do what she wants to do. She's not required to go on retreats, lead a small group, play the piano, or teach Sunday School. But if she wants to do one of those activities and feels that it is God's calling, I want her to follow through.

There are three things Robanne and I do to keep our marriage alive. First, we continue to date each other. One of the things missing in our marriage for many years was time spent together. Sure, we lived with each other, but we weren't dating each other any more.

One year on Valentine's Day, Robanne decided to do something special for me. All week long she kept giving me flowers, balloons, and cards that said, "Something special is going to happen on Valentine's Day."

On Valentine's Day, I spent part of the afternoon going around collecting clues for our clandestine meeting. I finally ended up on a train heading south to a town called Del Mar, where Robanne met me for dinner. It was a delightful date, and I felt like we celebrated the romance of marriage.

The second thing we do to keep our marriage alive is talk to each other. I spend a lot of time talking and planning with a lot of people, but in the past I rarely did that with my family. So Robanne and I now have a weekly business meeting where we sit down and talk about what we're reading, what we're thinking about, our plans for the future, how our children are doing, and so on.

This meeting needs to take place during hours that are not stressful for either of us. We usually go to lunch together so we're not tired and can talk in a normal way. I like to ask Robanne, "How are we getting along?" Marriage, like youth ministry, ebbs and flows. Sometimes it's good and sometimes it's not so good. Sometimes it's strong, and sometimes we need to ask questions about why we're feeling what we're feeling.

The third thing we do to keep our marriage alive is dream together. Robanne and I dream about what we want our family to be like. Recently we've been talking about where we'd like to live, what we want out of our lifestyle, and how we could change it. We need time to talk and dream together. Sometimes we go for long walks along the harbor down by our home. (My son R.W. likes to ride his bike while we dream about his future.)

Children

Robanne and I waited 11½ years before we had our first child. During that time of childless marriage, I always thought of parents as problems because they asked too many questions.

That all changed at 11:34 A.M. on October 24, 1985, when R.W. came into the world. Now I understand more than ever why parents get uptight about me taking their kids to Mexico. They worry about things that could go wrong, or about whether their son or daughter will get hurt on the rock-climbing trip.

The biggest problem that I had before the birth of R.W. was a lack of understanding about the responsibility that comes with parenting. Because I'm a parent now, I understand more fully how precious kids are to their families and why parents experience anxiety about them.

So how do I effectively involve my children in ministry?

Having a son has helped me to be a better youth pastor. Now I understand a little more about what kids go through in their relationships with their parents. I know there are many successful youth pastors who are unmarried or who do not have children. But becoming a father allowed me to have greater empathy toward parents.

I hurt with parents where I didn't before. When Janice's parents asked me to sit in on a briefing at her high school, I felt very privileged. When the school psychologist told us that Janice was mildly retarded and would never be able to graduate from that school, I forgot about feeling honored and cried with those parents. Thanks to R.W.'s entrance into my life, when parents come to me with problems, I can empathize and share in their pain instead of just feeling bad for them.

Parenting has also helped me speak with authority. I'm able to help students understand their parents' love. I've become closer to parents, putting them in support structures within my ministry.

Calendaring

When I think back on the last 10 arguments that Robanne and I have had, they have all originated from a circumstance where I knew something Robanne didn't know. One time I scheduled people for dinner but forgot to tell her until two or three hours before they arrived. That afternoon I called Robanne to see how dinner was coming along for the two sets of parents I had invited over three weeks earlier. Our conversation turned cool when I realized that I had not told her about this engagement. She had about 40 minutes to clean the house and prepare a meal!

Although Robanne was very polite and gracious during the evening, I realized a big showdown was coming when our guests left and the evening was over. The problem was lack of communication.

So how do I communicate my schedule to my family?

Robanne and I have designed a system where I give her my calendar on a weekly basis so she knows exactly what I've written in there. I also give her the authority to write on my schedule things that are important to our family. There is a day in my book right now that has "Disneyland" written all the way across it. Robanne wanted to make sure I didn't schedule anything else for that day.

Calendaring takes so little time but can create so many conflicts if you don't do it correctly. I do all my record-keeping on my home computer, and Robanne uses it to access my schedule whenever she needs to.

Family Budgets

At a National Youth Workers Conference, I met with a couple who live in a very affluent area of northern California. This couple is highly trained, has some wonderful ministry experiences, and would be an asset to anybody's staff. They had been involved in youth ministry at their church for five years.

When I asked them about their biggest problem in ministry, they immediately replied, "Finances!"

The church was underpaying this couple so much that the youth pastor had to work at a gas station part-time in order to make a living. What they did to solve that problem is a model for us all. They decided to keep accurate records of how they spent all their money for six months. They wrote down every dime they spent.

At the end of that six months, they made an appointment with one of the elders in the church who was their liaison in charge of finances. They told him, "Here's what we get paid from the church, and here's how we spent our money this last six months." The man was overwhelmed with how thrifty and how underpaid these people were. Three months later, they got a raise that greatly improved their family budget.

So how do I deal with family finances?

I really believe that problems with family finances are caused by two things:

1. Not having accurate information to ask the church for an adequate salary.

2. Not having an appropriate family budget so that money is spent in indiscriminate ways, resulting in financial difficulties.

One of my professors in college told Robanne and me about 10 years ago that we should live on 80% of our income, tithe 10%, and save 10%. As we use that system, we realize how wise it is. The 10% we save gives us the reserves to make courageous financial decisions. Since we started the Center for Student Missions, Robanne and I have been living by faith and the support of our friends.

I'm not sure we'll ever go back to earning a salary. Having to raise our own support has caused us to trust in the Lord's provision more than ever before. It's been good for our family.

Small Church Spotlight

Over the years, my husband, Stan, and I have delayed having
children because we thought a family would change, or perhaps
end, our ministry with youth as well as other goals we had for
our lives. In addition, many students have told us that they
think of us as their "surrogate parents."

Now, after a short round with cancer, I've lost the opportunity
to bear a child. And though I love some of my youth group members as if they were my own, I know they can never be an adequate substitute for a true parent/child relationship.

Whether Stan and I adopt or remain childless, I must continue looking to God for direction and guidance. Certainly there
are aspects of my ministry—having students constantly in our
home, going on trips, attending multiple weekly activities, and
so on—that would cease if I had a child. On the other hand, I'm
sure that being a parent would make me a different or perhaps
better youth worker.

The key for all youth workers is to listen to God's calling for every part of our lives. I don't believe He asks us to substitute ministry for marital or family relationships. Yet He does have a plan for our careers and personal lives, and He expects us to be obedient to Him as He reveals that plan.

Scripture Meditation

"If anyone sets his heart on being an overseer, he desires a noble task. Now the overseer must be above reproach, the husband of but one wife, temperate, self-controlled, respectable, hospitable, able to teach, not given to drunkenness, not violent but gentle, not quarrelsome, not a lover of money. He must manage his own family well and see that his children obey him with proper respect. (If anyone does not know how to manage his own family, how can he take care of God's church?)" (1 Timothy 3:1-5).

Spend some time meditating on what God has to say to you. Use the following questions to study this passage.

1. Why do you think Paul gave Timothy this list of qualifications for leadership instead of talking about the duties involved?

2. In what ways are you an overseer?

3. Does Paul's reference, "the husband of but one wife," imply that overseers or leaders must not be single?

4. If you are married, what grade would your spouse give you for managing your family? If you have children, how would they rate you?

5. Are there areas of your family life that have been neglected? If so, what can you do to rectify the situation?

Father, create within me a commitment to the spiritual leadership of my family as well as to my students.

COMPETITION

You and Competition

We didn't survey youth workers on competition, but because this is such a big issue for both of us, and the sources of competition are easily recognizable—any person, church, or organization that youth workers think may threaten their ministry—we decided to include this chapter.

So as you read about the competitiveness that Ridge sometimes experiences, ask yourself:

➤ Who or what is my biggest source of competition?

➤ How am I dealing with my competitiveness?

➤ How is my competitiveness harming my ministry?

Youth Workers Speak:

"The thing I like least about youth work is the competition and lack of cooperation between youth workers in different churches."

When I think back on my 15 years of youth ministry and how much energy I've wasted in competition, it disturbs me. I just can't always resist my feelings of competitiveness. I recognize that my problem is rooted in my own insecurities. For some mistaken reason, I think that I need to be perfect and well-rounded to be effective as a youth pastor. In order to be successful, I get the idea that I should have *all* the gifts of the Spirit as well as the fruit of the Spirit.

I've noticed that the people who threaten me most usually have strengths where I have weaknesses. Every hole in my youth program, every weakness I have, and every insecurity I feel is magnified by the person I am competing with. I'm embarrassed by my actions and thoughts and wonder why I can't seem to do better.

Other Youth Pastors

One of the things that I struggle with on a regular basis is competing with other youth workers. For some reason, I think I always have to be the best youth pastor, and have the biggest youth group or the newest ideas in order to be successful.

Part of the problem is my need to achieve status in the youth ministry world. Whenever youth workers got together in one city where I was ministering, I usually found myself strutting because I had the best facility in town with, the best gym and the coolest youth room. Even with those advantages, I was still a little bit envious that others had more money, more kids, and a nicer staff to work with. I was always afraid I was going to lose kids to other youth programs.

It bothers me that a kid in my youth group may go to a camp with another church. Why can't I look at the body of Christ as bigger than the church I serve? If a kid is going to be fed and grow more at another church, what's wrong with him or her going there?

So how do I deal with my competitiveness toward other youth pastors?

First of all, I need to rid myself of the tremendous pressure to be the biggest and best in town. I need to stop feeling as if I must have the kind of program that attracts more and more kids.

One of the ways that I have been able to get over some of these feelings is to be part of a youth pastors' fellowship. Of course, there's a lot of strutting that goes on at those meetings, but when I honestly share some of the feelings of hurt and the problems I have had in my youth ministry, others become more willing to share. I also find walls are broken down when youth pastors pray together and really seek God's guidance for the community, not just for their church's youth ministries.

More walls are broken down when the youth pastors and their wives get together. Often the wives seem less threatened by sharing their frustrations and find support from being together.

Parachurch Organizations

At one of the churches where I candidated, I was told, "There's a great parachurch program in town, and it meets at the county fairgrounds. It's the hottest youth ministry in the country, and we know you'll never be able to compete with that, but we want to make sure that you can work alongside them."

I checked out the program. There were a lot of church kids there mixing with unchurched kids (which I thought was wonderful). But the leader of the program had one line that really bothered me. He said, "Ridge, if the youth pastors in this town were doing the job, we wouldn't have to do things like this."

That statement irked me because the leader seemed to imply that his parachurch organization was somehow better, somehow more spiritual than youth ministries that the local churches were offering.

His attitude wasn't the only problem. This parachurch program was funded by the youth programs and the budgets of the churches in town. Not only was there competition for kids, but there was also competition for dollars, as many of the parents in our youth group supported the parachurch program on a regular basis.

This situation provided some very difficult moments in my opening days of ministry. I viewed this parachurch program as a potential kid stealer. They always seemed to have the best speakers, the best programs, the brightest camps. They also seemed to attract my best kids and take them away on retreats that exhausted their resources for going on my little church retreats.

I resented the fact that parachurch groups invited me to lunch and then asked me how I could help them accomplish *their* ministry. I even resented the fact that part of their mission statement was to bring kids into the local church, when I never saw their staff involved at that level.

Five years later, this particular parachurch program was almost nonexistent. The people who were running the program decided that this ministry was getting too large for them to handle. The positive side of its demise was that I was able to turn my kids' attention more toward their church family through missions projects and vision building. I'm not an evangelist or a particularly good Bible teacher, but I am good at motivation and enthusiasm. But with this parachurch program gone, we became such a discipleship-oriented community that we lost some of our effectiveness in evangelizing youth.

So how do I deal with my competitiveness toward parachurch organizations?

I have really wrestled with how to handle parachurch organizations that are pulling away kids from my youth ministry. My competitiveness toward the local parachurch program was precipitated by the idea that there weren't enough kids to go around. We were all striving to get the 10% of the high school kids who were interested in God to come to our programs instead of worrying about the 90% who weren't spiritually involved. Deep down, that competition really bothered me.

I believe the only way to deal with this competitiveness is to build relationships with the leaders of parachurch organizations. When I compete with the leaders of a parachurch organization, I usually find out that we are both insecure and distrustful of each another. But if we begin to build friendships and work on the common task of reaching kids, that competitive spirit begins to diminish.

At one of my churches, I shared an intern with Campus Life. That intern worked in the Campus Life club program and then used my youth program to bring kids into the church. Church partnership programs are a great way to bring an end to competition.

Volunteers

It seems odd to say that I have competed for status with my own volunteer staff. But those young volunteers could play basketball and rock-climb better than I could. They could relate better to kids because they knew more about music and favorite rock groups. Suddenly they became not a group of people who helped me do youth ministry, but a group who knew the kids better than I did, even though *I* was the paid professional.

Most people wouldn't have noticed that I had these feelings of rivalry from time to time. But deep down in my own spirit, I realized I was competing with my staff, and I felt a little inadequate to serve them even though they looked to me as their leader.

So how do I avoid competition with my volunteers?

Again, competition begins to diminish when we build good relationships with others. I try to build better relationships with volunteers by:

1. Providing them with training. One of the ways I reduced competition with volunteers was to go to seminars with them and learn together as much as we could. There's something about being in a learning situation together that strengthens relationships.

2. Encouraging them. One of the ways I encourage adult volunteers is by spending some time with them at their place of employment. I see what their work routine is like. The day I visited one of my volunteers who worked with physically-impaired children, I gained a whole new appreciation for her ability to empathize with her students.

3. Building a team. One of the best ways to recruit volunteers is to have volunteers recruit their friends. There's a sense of community that comes when people of like mind get together to accomplish ministry.

4. Making sure that team is eclectic. I try to make sure the team is made up of diverse personalities. They shouldn't all be just like me. I remember one of my teams was made up of a 60-year-old man and an 18-year-old graduate. This diversity seemed to create a great opportunity for kids to relate to one or more members of the team. It also reduced the amount of competition because we knew that while we were all different, we all had complementary talents and abilities.

Big Names and Programs

There seems to be an unwritten law that the youth workers who are really successful are the ones whose faces appear on brochures, book covers, and magazine covers. I've always been a little threatened by and competitive with those big names and big programs that come into town to do concerts or large youth rallies.

I was afraid if my kids participated in these big programs and heard these great speakers, they might want to go to another youth group. Even if I invited a well-known speaker to my own retreat or special event, I felt a little threatened by him or her. I had to show this person I was really valuable to my kids. The cause for this display is my unquenchable thirst for status. And that status is defined by other youth workers. I want to be recognized. I want to be the one who is asked to pray. I want to lead the committee. I want to be asked to head up the organization. It's my ego and my own quest for status that causes me to compete.

Now that I've written a few books and am on the road doing a fair amount of speaking, I know how empty that status really is. Although there are some benefits that come with being a public figure, a loneliness settles in from missing the relationships that I used to have in the local church.

So how do I avoid competitiveness with big names?

I need to pray for the people I feel I'm competing with. They don't have to be physical enemies; they could be enemies of the mind. When I pray for those people, I suddenly become an ally with them. Prayer changes my view of them. God softens my heart and helps me realize how wrong my attitude is.

There are three things I need to remember:

1. I need to know my call—mainly, that I've been called to a local church ministry. Just because a person talks to more people and spends more time in bigger youth programs does not mean he or she has a more important ministry. The issue is: Who is really reaching kids for Christ?

2. I need to know my limitations. As I get older, I need to understand that there are some things I just can't do. If I understand my limitations, I can ask God to help me appreciate people who can go beyond my limitations.

3. I need to know my own pride. The reason I resent some of the big-name people who come in and get my kids to do things that I can't get them to do is because I let my pride get in the way. I want my name mentioned, my picture on the poster, and so on.

Small Church Spotlight

In a small church, competition is a big issue. My small youth program must compete with larger churches, well-funded youth programs, and parachurch organizations. But the area where I feel the most competition is in dealing with the coaching and teaching staffs of the high schools in my community.

I feel as if the kids in my youth group are constantly weighing the events and programs I plan for them against the events planned by school administrators. Since many of the kids with whom I work are unchurched, their parents almost always insist that they make school-sponsored events their top priority. I recall being furious when the football coach decided to require my sophomore guys to miss our entire fall retreat because he wanted them to sit on the sidelines of Saturday's game and cheer for the varsity team.

It's not that I don't understand loyalty and team spirit. I just wish I was able to generate that same kind of loyalty and spirit in my youth group. So instead of working toward that goal, I usually fume, gripe, and resent teachers and administrators who seem to be interfering with my calendar of events.

Obviously, fuming, griping, and building up resentment will not help me feel less competitive, so this past year I decided to do two things to decrease my competitiveness. First, I made a commitment to attend as many sports events where I had students participating as I possibly could. This was not an easy task. Every Saturday for three months I could be found in the stands watching not just the varsity football game, but the freshman/sophomore game as well.

What I discovered is that not many parents were supporting their kids at the games. No wonder the kids valued their teachers and coaches! At least *they* were at the games! But I also found that my presence at the games didn't go unnoticed. In this small community, any sign of support for kids is appreciated.

The few parents who attended games began inviting me to sit with them. They asked me how the youth group was doing and told me how much they appreciated my support of their kids. A few weeks later, they introduced me to some of the teachers in the crowd. And when the kids became comfortable with me on their turf, they introduced me to some of their coaches. I began to get comments such as, "Oh, you work with the youth over at Lisle Bible Church, don't you?" and "I've heard your name mentioned at the Concerned Parents and Teachers Association."

This major time investment communicated to the kids in my group, their parents, and their coaches that I was just as committed to those kids as any of the school staff. I began to feel less threatened as I raised my visibility with the parents and school staff. When I realized that these people knew who I was and respected my ministry, my defenses went down and I determined to find ways to work with the school staff rather than fume, gripe, and criticize.

Scripture Meditation

"If anyone thinks he is something when he is nothing, he deceives himself. Each one should test his own actions. Then he can take pride in himself, without comparing himself to somebody else, for each one should carry his own load" (Galatians 6:3-5).

Spend some time meditating on what God has to say to you. Use the following questions to study this passage.

1. Does Paul contradict himself in this passage when he first asks that we deflate our grandiosity and then urges us to take credit for our accomplishments?

2. How can we find a balance between false pride and self-condemnation?

3. How do these two extremes affect our sense of competitiveness?

4. How dependent are you on the approval of others?

5. How can we rid ourselves of resentment toward those who seem to achieve more than we do?

Father, help me to put my trust in You, because You can cleanse me from harmful resentments and self-condemnation.

CHAPTER 10

THE FUTURE

You and the Future

How long have you been involved in youth ministry?

14%	Currently in first year
20%	1–2 years
15%	3–4 years
25%	5–10 years
26%	More than 10 years

What are your career plans for the future?

64%	Continue with youth ministry indefinitely
12%	Move into some other area of ministry
1%	Eventually transfer into a secular line of work
11%	Other
11%	Undecided

Figures have been rounded to the nearest whole percentage.

Summary

Though some sources tell us that the average youth worker has been in youth ministry almost nine years,[4] those who responded to this survey varied in experience. As these youth workers looked toward their future, 64% saw their responsibilities remaining with youth ministry.

As you contemplate your future in youth ministry, take notice of the suggestions Ridge shares about flexibility in ministry and career planning. As you check out this chapter, ask yourself:

➤ Is God still calling me to a ministry with youth?

➤ How satisfied am I with my job and ministry?

➤ What are the major reasons why I would consider leaving youth ministry?

Youth Workers Speak:

"I've begun to consider the real possibility of being in youth ministry for a lifetime. As long as God calls me to youth work, I'll be in it."

The nature of youth ministry will be changing as the baby boomer generation sends their kids to junior high and high school. We will see a return to traditional values. I see it in my own community. When I first moved to Dana Point, a beach community in southern California, the big issues were traffic and affordable housing. When I went down to the harbor on Sunday afternoon, I saw a lot of couples on roller skates, women dressed in shorts and bikini tops, and guys in sweats. Now I can go down to the harbor and see the bikinis have been replaced by baggy sweatshirts, the roller skates have become roller blades, and the couples are now pushing strollers.

Nowadays parents are concerned about parks, recreational programs for their children, and places for kids to ride bikes. According to a trendspotter in the *Chicago Tribune* (October 21, 1991), the big issues in the 1990s will be ethics, the environment, and education. Our society is returning to traditional family values. This means that the future for youth ministry is bright. People will select churches based on the kind of ministry offered to their kids and where they can receive the best Christian education. Youth ministry will have to be one of the main draws of the church in coming years.

Planning for the Future

Do I have a place in the future of youth ministry? When I look at people who have spent 30 years in youth ministry or say that they are committed for life, I wonder if I will ever make that commitment. I have a hard time staying with anything for more than about five years. In fact, I get bored with my life about every four or five years. I need to move or make some changes in order to stay interested in my job. Sometimes I have redecorated my house or changed responsibilities at work.

I'm pretty impressed by people who can stay at the same

church for 15 years. I was talking to Les Christie one day, who has been at his church for almost 20 years. He said that he has stayed as youth pastor for that many years primarily because he is involved in many different ministries of the church.

I'm not sure how long I will stay in youth ministry. And, frankly, I feel a little guilty about this. When I go to youth conferences, they tell me that youth ministry needs to be a lifelong calling. The only lifelong commitment I ever made was to Christ and to Robanne.

So how do I determine what role youth ministry plays in my future?

I depend on three things to keep my interest in youth ministry. First, I try new ideas each year. When I think I have my program organized in such a way to make my job easier, that's when I start to get bored and lose interest.

Second, I need to develop more of a family emphasis in my ministry. As I minister to more than one student from the same family, I've found that more ministry needs to be directed to the parents. I want to help families be stronger. That keeps me more attached to youth *ministry t*han the narrower focus of simply working with kids.

Finally, I need to recognize that my attention span is about four years. So sometimes when I feel like I'm getting restless, it could be that I need to change my emphasis in ministry, not change churches.

Concerns for the Future

When I think about what I will do 20 years from now, I don't have any great goals. I know there are people who can tell you 15 years ahead of time what they want to do, what they will be doing, and how they're going to do it. Managers and planners tell me that I should plan far in advance, but I just can't do that. It's not me. I'm a spontaneous, fairly impulsive person, and I want to be that kind of person the rest of my life.

Yet, as I head into my 40s, there are some things that influence how I look at the future. I'm more prone now to self-evaluation than when I was in my 20s. I'm more willing to look at myself and admit I'm good at this, I'm not good at other things, and I will never be able to do certain things. I guess I'm more comfortable with where I'm at in my walk with God and in my career. I find it a lot easier in my late 30s to evaluate myself than when I was in my 20s.

I also have some family concerns. I want what I do with my life to make me a better father and husband. I want my children to grow up in an environment that is healthy for them. My family has become a bigger priority than the youth program now that I'm a father.

I am also concerned about getting older. There are some things I just can't do with kids anymore. I don't want to climb the mountain just because it's there. I don't want to canoe for two weeks and eat freeze-dried food. I want a calmer, saner lifestyle.

So how do I deal with these concerns for the future?

I recognize my concerns limit my ability to do certain things in youth ministry. However, I also believe that if I want to stay in youth ministry, I can. There is a place for me as a 50-year-old youth pastor. It just means I need to be selective about the place and the time I involve myself in that kind of ministry.

If I stay in youth ministry, I have to change my approach to students. I would need to build a strong young staff that I can disciple. I could delegate the responsibilities for students through that staff so they become the front line of the youth ministry. In effect I would become a resource person and pastor to the youth staff.

Finally, I also recognize that if I stay in ministry, I must have broader interests than just youth ministry. I need to have influence within the church or within the youth ministry world on a national or regional basis. As I look around the country, the people who stay in youth ministry a long time also have broader interests than simply working with kids at a local church level. They are speakers and writers, or they're involved in a preaching and teaching ministry to a church on a regular basis.

Churches without Futures

One of the most depressing things I deal with are youth pastors whose successful youth ministries are hindered because their churches have no vision for kids. When I came to my first church, I really believed I would be there for the rest of my life. But there came a day when the church voted down a building program that I knew was important if we were going to stick together as a staff. When they vetoed that program, I knew my days at the church were numbered. We were a staff of dreamers in a church comfortable with the status quo. Had we stayed, we would have ended up causing conflict.

So how do I deal with a church that has no future?

It was difficult to work after I realized that I didn't have a future at that church. But I've realized there are some characteristics of a church without a future. First of all, I steer clear of a senior pastor who doesn't care about growth but likes the idea of hiring an ambitious youth worker. I've found that when the senior pastor has no vision, he will not allow the youth worker to have a vision.

Recently I talked with a youth worker from a large church in San Antonio who was serving with a senior pastor four years away from retirement. The youth worker recognized that his church was going to be on hold for four years and had to ask himself a question: *Do I want to spend the next four years of my life in this situation and then maybe another two years looking for a new pastor and adjusting to his style?* The answer for that person was no. That church may have had a future, but the youth worker realized the staff did not. Youth work can be done in a church that has no commitment to growth, but the person who runs such a maintenance ministry must learn to be satisfied with modest results.

Staff Changes

What do I do if my senior pastor resigns? Does that mean my ministry is over? Does that mean I no longer have a future at my church?

When my senior pastors have resigned, my first responses have been ones of insecurity. What will this mean to my family and to my future? I become unsure of the power structure of the church as well. I know that the way the staff relates to each other will change. People who once had little or no authority will become significant players during the transition period. I feel that it's a little unfair that I have to change the way *I* operate because of a staff change.

During the transition period I become easily distracted from my ministry. I begin to seize the opportunity to gain more influence in the church and do things that I usually wouldn't be interested in at all, such as preaching, attending board meetings, and getting involved in the polity of the church. I've been noticing that more and more youth pastors seem to leave youth ministry during the time of transition between pastorates. Perhaps like me they become insecure and distracted.

So how do I respond to staff changes?

As an associate staff person, I need to recognize a couple of things when my senior pastor resigns. First, until the new senior pastor takes his place, and probably six months after he comes on board, my ministry becomes the job of holding the church together instead of helping it to grow and expand.

Second, I need to broaden my ministry base to help the church during this time of transition. There are things that I will be asked to do during those times that I might not be asked to do if the church had a senior pastor. For example, I might be asked to preach, counsel, be in elders' meetings, and make larger financial decisions for the church. I can view this as a great opportunity to learn new aspects of ministry.

I can also use this time to tap into unused gifts as opportunities to speak and be in charge of services arise, duties that perhaps I would not have been asked to do before.

I may also need to offer my resignation. It's very important to realize that I work not only for the government of the church and for the congregation, but that I am also directly linked to the administration of the previous senior pastor. As a courtesy, I may need to offer my resignation to the new senior pastor, effective at his installation. Then he can decide to accept or reject that resignation.

The new senior pastor may decide to continue a relationship with me on a trial basis so that both of us have a chance to either get out of our relationship in a graceful way or confirm our commitment to a long-standing ministry.

When It's Time to Resign

I remember the day that I resigned from my first church. It was one of the saddest days of my life as I realized I was leaving a big part of my heart at that church. I wasn't just resigning from a job; Robanne and I were pulling away from some of the most important relationships in our lives.

Resigning is never an easy decision, especially if you're not sure how the staff, congregation, or youth group will respond. When some people learn that you're leaving, they feel betrayed and treat you accordingly. So your heart is broken not only because you are leaving intimate friends, but because of the hurt and pain some people feel over your resignation.

So how do I know when it's time to leave?

I believe God prepared me to leave all the places that I've left. Through those experiences I've drawn up a list of 13 characteristics that were true of my life when it was time to leave:

1. God revealed to me through His Word and through prayer that He was making me restless and that it was time to move on.

2. I got bored and frustrated. I stopped enjoying my job and ministry. Things that were so easy for me just months earlier suddenly became dull and burdensome.

3. I started to meddle in church business where I had no right to meddle. At one church, I became very concerned about the kind of copy machine we were going to purchase. It was an issue that I had shown no interest in during the previous two years.

4. I was troubled by the overall direction of the church.

5. I had personality conflicts. I began to have trouble with people on staff or those I worked with.

6. Other job possibilities came my way. God brought a phone call or a letter that gave me the opportunity to leave the church and go somewhere else.

7. I was not growing spiritually. My spiritual life was dry, and God became distant. I began to see that ministry was being done out of my own spirit, not out of the Spirit of God.

8. I worried about things. I worried about the finances of the church, about my direction in ministry, about things that might

not have even happened. I worried about impending meetings and the decisions that would be made.

9. I withdrew or I talked too much. I was Dr. Jekyll and Mr. Hyde. At one church where I was ready to leave, I dominated every staff meeting with chitchat. At another church, I withdrew and just sort of put in my time.

10. I strutted. I began talking about all the great things I had done instead of concentrating on problems and solutions. I made sure I looked real good.

11. Those in authority told me my ministry was over. I've watched lots of youth ministers across the country fight with elders who tell them it's time to move on. If the elders of the church placed in authority over me tell me that my ministry is over, I can be sure that it's God's will.

12. My friends told me that it was time to leave. When I developed the right kind of accountability with the right kinds of friends, I found that they were honest with me. They could tell me that it might be time for me to find another place to minister.

13. I knew when it was time to leave, because deep in my heart God gave me peace about relocating.

When do I know it's time to leave? When eight or more of these symptoms have occurred, it's time for me to think about the future.

Small Church Spotlight

"By the time 2000 arrives, the majority of the youth in America will be in their teens."[5] George Barna feels the church must shift its resources from reaching children to reaching teenagers.[6] I believe the church needs to respond to this advice in three ways:

1. Worship. Kids desire to feel God, to touch Him, to become emotionally involved with Him. Therefore, I think youth in the future will be looking for opportunities to worship. Such times may not include "singing" types of worship, but simply intimate times with God. That means our Sunday morning worship services will be crucial in recruiting young people.

2. Service opportunities. Kids want to feel significant, that they can make a difference in this world. Thus, missions and service will be very important to youth ministry. Organizations like the Center for Student Missions will be offering more opportunities for youth missions experiences. And more and more youth workers will be taking on the challenge of getting their students involved in service to the homeless, the disabled, the elderly, neglected children, and other hurting people.

3. Caring ministries. Kids are looking for a place where people care about them. Every kid needs an adult to be crazy about him or her. Parents and schools aren't taking care of this need, and in some cases, neither are churches. Youth workers will hear from more single parent families about the need for big brother/buddy programs for teenagers. In turn, we may be able to help students give this care back to younger children in the form of latchkey and child-care programs.

Scripture Meditation

"'For I know the plans I have for you,' declares the Lord, 'plans to prosper you and not to harm you, plans to give you hope and a future. Then you will call upon me and come and pray to me, and I will listen to you. You will seek me and find me when you seek me with all your heart'" (Jeremiah 29:11-13).

Spend some time meditating on what God has to say to you. Use the following questions to study this passage.

1. What conclusions about God's power can you draw from these verses?

2. List the promises God made to the exiles in this passage.

3. Do you ever wonder what God has planned for your future?

4. What does God expect from us as we seek to make plans for our future?

5. What hope has God given you in regard to your ministry? Your personal life? Your family? Your students?

Father, help me to seek you with all my heart as I look to the future.

1. " Today's Teens: A Generation in Transition," Barna Research Group, Glendale, Calif., 1990.

2. Ibid.

3. Kate Greer, "Today's Parents: How Well Are They Doing?" *Better Homes and Gardens,* October 1986, 36-46.

4. Unpublished survey of 140 *GROUP* Magazine readers, 1987, in *The Youth Ministry Resource Boook,* Eugene C. Roehlkepartain, ed. (Loveland, Colo.: Thom Schultz Publications, 1988), p. 184.

5. George Barna, *The Frog in the Kettle* (Ventura, Calif.: Regal Books, 1990), p. 205.

6. "Today's Teens: A Generation in Transition," Barna Research Group, 1990.

BIBLIOGRAPHY

Chapter 1 STUDENTS

Anthony, T. Mitchel, *Suicide: Knowing When Your Teen Is at Risk*. Ventura, Calif.: Regal, 1992.
This book will help you recognize the warnings of teenage suicide and offers practical counsel for those helping suicidal teens.

Rowley, William J. *Equipped to Care: A Youth Worker's Guide to Counseling Teenagers*. Wheaton, Ill.: Victor Books, 1990.
Addresses adolescent development, building relationships with teenagers, and crisis intervention.

"Today's Teens: A Generation in Transition." Barna Research Group, Glendale, Calif., 1990.

Veerman, David. *Reaching Out to Troubled Youth*. Wheaton, Ill.: Victor Books, 1987.
Talks about ways to minister to troubled youth, how to communicate and discipline, how to deal with substance abuse, child abuse, and homosexuality.

Chapter 2 SCHOOL AND COMMUNITY

Campolo, Tony, and Gordon Aeschliman. *50 Ways You Can Feed a Hungry World*. Downers Grove, Ill.: InterVarsity Press, 1991.
Fifty suggestions for people who want to do something about world hunger.

Schimmels, Cliff. *Parents' Most-Asked Questions about Kids and Schools.* Wheaton, Ill.: Victor Books, 1989.

Temple, Gray, Jr. *52 Ways to Help Homeless People.* Nashville, Tenn.: Thomas Nelson, 1991.
Practical ways to make a measurable impact on your community.

Chapter 3 CHURCH STAFF AND CONGREGATION
Burns, Ridge, and Pam Campbell. *Create in Me a Youth Ministry.* Wheaton, Ill.: Victor Books, 1986.
Candid sharing of experiences in youth ministry. See especially chapters 8 and 9.

Van Auken, Phillip M. *The Well-Managed Ministry.* Wheaton, Ill.: Victor Books, 1989.
Workbook for developing consistent management styles in Christian organizations.

Chapter 4 PARENTS
Dockrey, Karen. *Youth Workers and Parents: Sharing Resources for Equipping Youth.* Wheaton, Ill.: Victor Books, 1990.

Greer, Kate. "Today's Parents: How Well Are They Doing?" *Better Homes and Gardens,* October 1986, 36–46.

Rice, Wayne, and Ken Davis. *Understanding Your Teenager.* Grand Rapids, Mich.: Zondervan, 1992.
A six-session video curriculum helping parents and teens build better relationships.

Chapter 5 PERSONAL ISSUES

Bertolini, Dewey M. *Back to the Heart of Youth Work*. Wheaton,
Ill.: Victor Books, 1989.
How to develop proven character, a biblical philosophy of
ministry, and a practical methodology.

Hemfelt, Dr. Robert, Dr. Frank Minirth, and Dr. Paul Meier.
Love Is a Choice. Nashville, Tenn.: Thomas Nelson, 1991.
Explores the causes of codependency and how the uncon-
ditional love of God is an essential step in the healing process.

Kageler, Len. *The Youth Minister's Survivial Guide*. Grand
Rapids, Mich.: Zondervan, 1992.
Case studies of over 100 fired youth workers. How to rec-
ognize and overcome the hazards you will face.

Chapter 6 PROGRAMS

Dickie, Steve, and Darrell Pearson. *Creative Programming
Ideas for Junior High Ministry*. Grand Rapids, Mich.: Zondervan, 1992.
Easy-to-use ideas for youth meetings, Sunday School,
camps and retreats, music and drama, recreation, and
much more.

Karen Dockrey, *The Youth Worker's Guide to Creative Bible
Study*. Wheaton, Ill.: Victor Books, 1991.
Fresh ideas for keeping youth involved in Bible study.

Chapter 7 YOUTH GROUPS

Robbins, Duffy. *Youth Ministry That Works*. Wheaton, Ill.: Victor Books, 1991.
Six essentials for hands-on ministry and discipleship.

St. Clair, Barry. The Moving Toward Maturity series. Includes five titles: *Following Jesus, Spending Time Alone with God, Making Jesus Lord, Giving Away Your Faith,* and *Influencing Your World,* as well as a leader's guide (*Moving Toward Maturity Leader's Book*) and a leadership training workbook (*Building Leaders for Strategic Youth Ministry*). Wheaton, Ill.: Victor Books, 1991.

Chapter 8 FAMILY

Arterburn, Stephen, and Carl Dreizler. *52 Simple Ways to Say "I Love You."* Nashville, Tenn.: Thomas Nelson, 1991.
Fun and fresh ideas for telling people in unique ways that you love them.

Dettoni, John, and Carol Dettoni. *Parenting Before and After Work.* Wheaton, Ill.: Victor Books, 1992.
Making the most of your family's time together.

Dreizler, Carl. *52 Simple Ways to Have Fun with Your Child.* Nashville, Tenn.: Thomas Nelson, 1991.
Quick ideas for fun that will help develop a parent-child bond.

Fields, Doug. *Creative Romance.* Eugene, Ore.: Harvest House, 1991.
Practical ideas to help spouses keep the sizzle in their love.

Wright, Don. *How to Plan a Trip the Whole Family Will Enjoy.* Elkhart, Ind.: Cottage Publications, 1992.

Chapter 9 COMPETITION

Hemfelt, Dr. Robert, Dr. Frank Minirth, and Dr. Paul Meier. *We Are Driven.* Nashville, Tenn.: Thomas Nelson, 1991.
The compulsive behaviors that cause us to need to do more and be more.

Mains, David. *Healing the Dysfunctional Church Family.* Wheaton, Ill.: Victor Books, 1992.
See especially chapter 3.

Chapter 10 THE FUTURE

Barna, George. *The Frog in the Kettle.* Ventura, Calif.: Regal, 1990.

Barna, George. *What Americans Believe.* Ventura, Calif.: Regal, 1991.
An annual survey of values and religious views in the United States.

Chandler, Russell. *Racing Toward 2001.* Grand Rapids, Mich.: Zondervan, 1992.
The forces shaping America's religious future.

Roehlkepartain, Eugene C., ed. *The Youth Ministry Resource Book.* Loveland, Colo.: Thom Schultz Publications, 1988.
Read the unpublished survey of 140 *GROUP* Magazine readers, 1987, found on p. 184.

Senter, Mark, III. *The Coming Revolution in Youth Ministry.* Wheaton, Ill.: Victor Books, 1992.
Traces the forces that shaped past youth ministry, analyzes present social and global trends, and—based on this decade's megatrends—predicts what the youth ministry revolution will look like.

"Today's Teens: A Generation in Transition." Barna Research
Group, Glendale, Calif., 1990.

INDEX